"No surprise here: *What You Didn't Learn from Your Parents About Sex* is another delightfully quirky Matthew Paul Turner book that had me laughing out loud and learning something along the way. Matthew's honesty and healthy view of sex made this book a whimsical, informative, and helpful read. I wish every college student and young engaged couple would read this book."

—CAMERON CONANT, author of *With or Without You: A Spiritual Journey Through Love and Divorce* and the forthcoming *The Year I Got Everything I Wanted*

"Matthew's book helped me overcome my unhealthy addiction to Justin Timberlake. It can do that and more for you."

—anonymous Christian rock star

W9-BTF-109

what you didn't learn from your parents about

sex

[a guide to a touchy subject]

matthew paul turner

TH1NK
P.O. Box 35001
Colorado Springs, Colorado 80935

ISBN 1-57683-940-0

Cover design by Brand Navigation, LLC: DeAnna Pierce, Terra Petersen, and Bill
Chiaravalle, www.brandnavigation.com
Cover photo by iStock, Stan Rohrer
Creative Team: Nicci Hubert, Kathy Mosier, Arvid Wallen, Laura Spray, Pat Reinheimer

Some of the anecdotal illustrations in this book are true to life and are included with the
permission of the persons involved. All other illustrations are composites of real situations, and any resemblance to people living or dead is coincidental.

Turner, Matthew Paul, 1973-
  What you didn't learn from your parents about-- sex : a guide to a
touchy subject / Matthew Paul Turner.
    p. cm.
  Includes bibliographical references.
  ISBN 1-57683-940-0
  1. Sex--Religious aspects--Christianity. I. Title.
BT708.T87 2006
241'.66--dc22
                              2006018993

Printed in the United States of America

1 2 3 4 5 6 7 8 9 10 / 10 09 08 07 06

FOR A FREE CATALOG OF NAVPRESS BOOKS & BIBLE STUDIES, CALL
1-800-366-7788 (USA) OR 1-800-839-4769 (CANADA)

Contents

What You Didn't Learn From Your Parents Presents:
[rules for writing acknowledgments]

1. Always thank your spouse!

Jessica, thank you for your love, support, and passion. You probably never expected your name to be mentioned in so many books. Well, neither did I. I love you, baby. [Hint: Your spouse should always be either the first or last person you mention—if he or she is the first, God must be the last. If God's the first, put your spouse last. Hey, it's the rule!]

2. Mention the family!

You guys know I love you, right? Well, just in case you don't, Dad, Mom, Melanie, Kelley, Elisabeth, Jim, Kevin, David, Jillana, Jenna, Andrew, Katelyn, Layton, Emma, and Sierra—also Mom and Dad Schim and Melissa: I LOVE YOU! [Nieces and nephews: You're not allowed to read this book unless your mothers tell you it's okay. Mom and Dad: Read with caution!]

3. Don't forget to thank those who help you do what you do!

Rebekah, I'll always remember praying with you outside of Dalts—thank you for your friendship and wisdom. Valerie, I promise I don't "have" you. Tommy, thanks for driving! To everyone who let me use their stories or advice in this book, thank you. Daniel and Lisa, can you believe we've been friends now for almost seven years? Wow. You up for a few more? I am, but only if you guys are. . . .

4. Don't forget to acknowledge the organizations that lend you their support!

Lot of love goes out to World Vision, Nashville Speakers Bureau, and Maxx Productions.

5. NEVER FORGET YOUR PUBLISHER!

Nicci, thanks for letting me write a book about sex. I've always wanted to write a book about sex, and just like I expected, it was awesome—"ducking" awesome! [And A LOT of work.] You deserve a raise for putting up with me! Mel, thanks for thinking I'm funny. Kate, thank you for www.myspace.com/MPTBooks. Kathy, umm, well, you'll no doubt edit the sentence I'm writing right now, but knowing you, you'll probably make it much better. No, seriously, thank you for making me sound like a writer. Doug, thank you for Fleming and John and for your marketing expertise! Mike, thank you for believing in this project. And to everyone else at TH1NK and NavPress who will have anything to do with this series, thank you very much for sharing your talent with me. Joel Osteen says you'll prosper! But between you and me, that's up for debate.

6. Don't forget to thank GOD!

[I'm not sure God reads Christian nonfiction. So I'm not sure he'll see your thank you, but all of his followers are expecting it—and you have to keep them happy! Or at least try to.]

You now know how to write an acknowledgments page! But write the book first, okay?

Before We Begin . . .
[rules for reading this book]

Every Christian sex book has rules. Actually, it seems the more rules a Christian sex book has, the better it sells. That is a bit troubling to me. And since this book won't order you around [well, not as much as others], I thought it might be good to stick in a few rules at the beginning to boost its chances of becoming a best seller.

Rule #1: Listen. When you hear my voice, or at least what you believe to be my voice, talking inside your head, make sure you're listening closely. All of the stories, facts, and, of course, the advice have been written with you in mind. If you're not listening, my voice will be talking inside your head for no reason. And that might get lonely for me.

Rule #2: Grow. I'm convinced God is going to cause a great amount of growth in your life once you've read this book. If you fail to comply with the growth, your preacher might very well show up unannounced at your front door wearing nothing but a plastic baptistery smock.

Rule #3: Think. Sadly, we Christians often struggle with thinking about sex in a healthy and holy manner. A lot of us have views and perceptions about sex that are in need of a serious overhaul. This can't happen unless your mind is engaged in the process. That means you might have to use your mind while reading this book. But just a little, I promise.

Rule #4: Obey "aha" moments. Reading this book might cause you to experience a few "aha" moments. Of course, don't mistake "aha" moments with the "ha ha," "umm," and "huh?" moments you might also experience. "Aha" moments could mean God is speaking to you. If you feel him speaking, begin listening, growing, and thinking immediately.

Rule #5: Be honest. Resist the temptation to lie to yourself about your personal story. When thinking about your life in regard to sex, honesty is essential. You can't submit to God's plan if you aren't being honest about what truly is happening in your life.

Introduction
[in sex terms, this is the foreplay]

This book is about sex.

But you knew that; in fact, it probably was the topic that inspired you to pick up this curious little guidebook. Am I right? It's okay. You can be honest.

Let's face it: Who doesn't like reading books about sex? Well, okay, so I'm quite sure some Christians aren't so keen on it. But talking and thinking about sex shouldn't be considered abnormal; it's an exciting subject to discuss, one of adventure and intrigue, something Christians are meant to enjoy and not feel worried, nervous, or guilty about.

Our appetite for sex is kind of like a kid whose parents drive by a favorite ice-cream establishment. As soon as the kid sees the brightly colored Ben & Jerry's sign, he begins yelling, "Mommy, I want some ice cream! Can we please stop for some ice cream? I'm really hungry, Mom! Can we stop, Dad? Can we? PLEASE? OH, PLEASE? I REALLY NEED IT!"

Of course, this example isn't perfect, but you get the idea. I realize most Christians don't make a habit of screaming, "I WANT SOME SEX! I WANT SOME SEX!" At least, not when they're in the backseat of their parents' car. But admit it, my analogy isn't bad.

The excitement is no doubt similar. And if my example is off base in any way, it's because you believe a kid's excitement for ice cream pales in comparison to your excitement about sex. Am I right?

That's not a bad thing; in fact, it's normal. You should be excited about it. God wants us jumping up and down about it. Many Christian "sexperts"—yes, they do exist—call sex a gift from God. If that's true, then I believe it should be just like Christmas, but better. In other words, it should be a gift that is stimulating, hope-filled, electrifying, and seldom breaks.

Hopefully you've been aware for quite some time that your inner [and outer] excitement for sex is very much a normal part of being human. If you're not aware of this, you might want to revisit one of those kids' books on puberty, you know, the ones where they usually describe one's genitalia like that of a blossoming flower.* If you go back and read one of these books, you'll learn that sexual desire is a natural part of a human's DNA. You can't help but be a little excited about it.

---

*I recommend the children's books What's Happening to My Body? [for boys] and Changes in You and Me [for girls].

However, simply being aware that sexual desires are completely normal doesn't make feelings, especially the urges we experience prior to falling in love and getting married, any less complicated. For Christians, at least those who are attempting to live their lives as holy sacrifices [everyone sing with me!], these normal human desires often make life a little difficult, perhaps confusing, and sometimes even guilt ridden.

Believe me, I've experienced the difficult, confusing, and guilt-ridden struggle firsthand. I'm not sure if holy living was supposed to be this hard. I'm not sure pursuing holiness was meant to be difficult. But a lot of the time, at least for me, it's hard. Like Jolly Rancher hard.

Sadly, being a Christian engaged in the sometimes [perhaps oftentimes] insane world of evangelicalism does little to help the "holy" cause. In fact, I've often thought church culture, with all of its sex seminars, books, "experts," and small groups, makes knowing and living by God's design more difficult. It seems to me our "programs" often do little more than stifle people's ability to be honest and open about the sexual struggles they face.

However, this culture we reside in doesn't simply force us to shut down the issues. It also asphyxiates our ability to tap into the beauty and extraordinary thrill of sexual desire.

If it's truly "God's gift," why do most Christians feel disempowered by their surroundings? Too often, I meet Christians who, instead of celebrating holy sexuality with excitement, are much more focused on not crossing lines, the guilty feelings that happen when they screw up, and hoping no one ever finds out what they're like behind closed doors.

Of course, some Christians have endured more suffocation than others. I know Christians who were raised in environments where the word *penis* was forbidden unless spoken in a whisper. And even then, whispering it was only kosher for medical emergencies, you know, like red bumps, throbbing pain, or prolonged erections. Any conversation that didn't involve an itchy or achy annoyance was simply considered frivolous "sex talk."

I've got a secret for you. You might want to get a little closer. I think it might be best if I whisper this one to you.

This book is full of **FRIVOLOUS** sex talk!

[*Gasp!*]

Why would this book be filled with "frivolous" sex talk, you ask?

Because Christians need good discussions about sex and

sex-related topics, that's why. And we don't always need to be quite as protective of ourselves as we think.

I'm no sex expert.

It's shocking, I know.

In fact, if someone had told me I would someday write a sex book [especially one that is sometimes funny but also filled with advice, commentary, and personal stories], I would have laughed. My mother *did* laugh. However, she stopped laughing when I told her that the more she laughed, the more stories about her and Dad I would include. [She thought that was pretty funny.]

Anyway, despite not being a sex expert, I have learned a thing or two about it over the years, especially as it relates to Christians.

I've ventured through life as a Jesus-follower since I was four. When I turned eighteen, I truly believed that because I had never done *anything* remotely sexual, I had survived the toughest part of the "virginity journey." [Ha ha ha ha ha 😳] I thought for sure I'd go to college, find the love of my life, get married, and live a sexually thrilling existence for all of eternity. [Ha ha ha ha ha 😳]

Well, I am indeed married now, but that didn't happen until I was almost thirty-one. Yeah, so much for it being easy. In fact, the fifteen years I lived between thinking I was perfect and writing this book have been, at times, excruciating. They haven't been quite as bad as my wife making me sit through two hours of *The Girl with the Pearl Earring*, but trust me, they were hard. Honestly, in my search for the answers, I've fallen down more times than I can count.

I might as well tell you up front: This book doesn't have all the answers, but it certainly has some.

So as we discuss sex together, I pray you find some hope, some encouragement, and also a little bit of laughter. Enjoy this little book. If you've been a Christian for at least forty-seven seconds, you've probably earned it.

Oh yeah, don't share this book with your friends. Make them buy their own copies. This book is beginning to feel very attached to you.

Books have feelings, too.

Matthew
matthew@dottedline.net
www.matthewpaulturner.com
www.myspace.com/MPTBooks

WOW. I think I feel a second introduction coming on.

I know what you're thinking; you're thinking that a second intro-

duction is not possible for a writer in ONE book. But you're wrong. Some writers have learned how to master a second introduction. For me, a second introduction is really quite simple. However, I don't think this is the time or the place to be discussing my success in achieving second introductions. If you e-mail me, I will let you in on my secret.

More Frivolous Sex Talk . . .

I was just seven years old when I first heard the word *sex*. The little three-letter word was said out loud on a TV show called *The Facts of Life*. Some of you aren't familiar with this TV show. Well, unless you make a habit of watching TV Land.

Okay, Time For a Spontaneous Game

[expect a few spontaneous games throughout]

How many words can you write in the margins of this book using the letters *X*, *S*, and *E*? There's one rule: You have to use all of the letters at the same time.

Do-Do — Do-Do — Do-Do-Do/Do-Do — Do-Do-DO! *do do do do do* [*Jeopardy* theme song]

[The answer is at the bottom of this page, written in super-small font and spun upside down to make you turn this book 180 degrees to read it.]

ANSWER: Only one word can be made using these letters: sex. Easy, huh? Read this answer backwards and see if you can find the hidden message.

When I was little, my sisters and I loved the show. But a curious thing happened on one episode. The show named *The Facts of Life* actually began talking about "the facts of life." One evening, just as my father walked into the family room, Blair, played by the now-famous homeschooling mom Lisa Whelchel, uttered a sentence about sex to Tootie, played by the always delightful Kim Fields. Yes, her character name was Tootie. Hey, weird things were cool in the eighties, like spandex and Petra.

Upon hearing the "sex" sentence, my father jutted his jaw out from the rest of his mouth, and then he yelled, "MATTHEW! Turn that garbage off immediately!"

Dad rarely stopped after one command. His angst continued. "You know, Carole," he said, looking at my mom, who was making quiche in the kitchen, "I have a great mind to take that TV outside and put a shotgun hole right through it. I can't believe they put junk like that on TV."

"I wouldn't blame you, Virgil," said my mom, while beating eggs. "I certainly don't need it."

When my mother said this, my heart began racing. The thought of no TV scared my sisters and me to death.

My father had a serious love/hate relationship with our television. If it weren't for the news, sports, and a strange connection to any movie made with Clint Eastwood in it, I truly believe my house would have been TV-less.

As I looked at my dad, with an expression that said, *Please don't shoot the TV*, I realized then and there that sex was bad — really bad.

But "bad things" were nothing new. When I was seven, everything, at least everything remotely enjoyable to the human senses, was considered bad. In the church my family went to, unless a pleasure-filled action was Holy Spirit inspired, it was labeled "worldly behavior." And, in fact, even some Holy Spirit–motivated actions were off-limits.

However, despite my father's angst toward "sex talk" on TV, he did talk to me about sex once. And once was enough.

The time my father talked to me about sex was the longest fourteen minutes of my twelve-year-old life. After those fourteen minutes were over, sex was no longer just bad; it was now awkward, too.

But such is the case with parental sex talks. Sex talks make sex awkward for a lot of us. The "talk" is one of those experiences through which most people admit to learning one thing — they never again want to experience the humiliation of hearing their father or mother use the word *penis* that many times in one sitting *ever* again.

Perhaps you know the awkwardness I'm talking about. Every time my father would say the word *penis*, it was like a bomb was going off in my head. "Matthew, you have a *penis*." *BOOM!* "Sometimes your *penis* ..." *BOOM!* "When your *penis* ..." *BOOM!* In fact, by minute seven, *penis* became the only word I *could* hear other than the word *breasts*. For some reason, a boy, even a Christian boy, can't help but hear the word *breasts*.

I am certainly not the only person who was tortured by a parental sex talk. A lot of people have experienced them. The sex talks our parents put us through made most of us want to go running through the house, covering our ears, screaming "LA LA LA LA" in protest. No matter how cool and understanding parents are, engaging in sex chats with them is rarely, if ever, fun. At least not until you're married. After that, talking sex with your parents can be moderately tolerated—only because then you can bring up your GREAT sex life in front of them. "Yeah, Dad, last night Jess and I ..." *BOOM!*

I figure a little uncomfortable squirming won't hurt them. After all, they started it.

However, I have to admit that my attitude toward my sex talk has changed. Over the years, I have learned that my father, in the way he talked to me, was actually being rather easy on me. Our conversation was just that, a simple fourteen-minute talk. There were no "how to" books or poorly drawn illustrations or foreign instruments to help my father's sex lesson come alive in my young mind. I mean, he did use his hands once to help me visualize how the penis was made to fit into the vagina, but that was it. *Umm, that was enough.*

But for some kids, it wasn't that simple. Some Christian parents use "helpful tools" to help educate their kids about sex. "HELPFUL TOOLS?" I'm not lying about this.

I have a friend whose parents, in an effort to help explain what happens during intercourse, pulled out Abraham and Sarah "Barbie" dolls. *Yes.* Each of them held one of the robed dolls and proceeded to move through the actions of intimacy. They didn't stop the demonstration until both dolls were completely naked and lying next to each other on top of a pink Barbie bed.

Yeah, my friend told me the book of Genesis has never been quite the same.

"As a kid, I was never able to sing 'Father Abraham' in Sunday school without those darn dolls popping into my mind," he said to me.

But wait, it gets better [or worse, depending on your perspective].

One twentysomething told me her mom used a clothespin to illustrate the penis and an empty film container to represent the vagina. I didn't think anything about it, really; it wasn't all that different from my father using his hands. But this girl had a different opinion. "When I was ten, the clothespin and film container really helped me visualize the act of intercourse," she said. "It made me see how personal it was.* However, when I got married, I expected my husband's penis to be the same size as a clothespin. [*Oops!*] For two months, the size of his larger-than-I-had-imagined member made me cry."

I have been surprised to learn that many parents never talk to their kids about sex. A few years ago, this topic of "parental sex talks" interested me. In an effort to see how different my experience was from that of other young adults, I polled my friends to see how many of them had experienced at least one explanatory conversation about sex with their parents. I was shocked to learn that 50 percent of my thirty or so close friends had never had a parental sex talk.

---

* *I'm not sure how a clothespin and an old film container made it more "personal," but hey, that's what she said.*

Through that little unofficial survey, I realized I was blessed that my father cared enough to talk about sex with me. In fact, my realized blessing made me decide that it was time for me to go ahead and forgive Dad for the two years I spent thinking that a woman's sexual organ was called a fajita. Yes, a fajita. Of course, it's not like he said the word incorrectly; I just heard it wrong. But come on, he could have made sure I had the correct pronunciation. It's not like it was one of the "lesser known" pieces of the sexual puzzle. I get pretty embarrassed to think back at how many times I talked about "fajitas" with my friends in the locker room during those two years. Not to mention trips to Taco Bell—I got freaked out every time I saw the menu.

Although my dad did talk about sex with me, many parents do not. In all fairness, although it's not an excuse, the sex talk is probably very awkward for Christian moms and dads, especially those who have been subject to the harshness of the church. I believe it's safe to assume that the average conservative Christian mom doesn't wake up one morning and think to herself, "Oh, thank you, Jesus; today I get to tell my eleven-year-old daughter all about the outer and inner workings of her vagina. I can't wait!" And how many dads struggle making the transition from "Hey, son, did you get your fishing pole baited?" to "Speaking of baiting your pole, son, I need to chat with you about . . ."

As you can probably imagine, Christian parents have very different comfort levels when teaching sex to their kids. All of us encountered very different experiences. Some parents are very open and honest. Others are reserved. And others don't talk about sex at all. In fact, most Christian parents [though certainly not all] fit somewhere into the following five categories. See if your parents fit any of the five. Then place a check mark in the box next to the one that best fits your parents' style.

Five Types of Sex-Talking Christian Parents

❑ **The oversharers.** These parents tell their kids way too much about sex too early in life. These hippie-prone mavericks tend to let it all hang out at the most inappropriate times. Their children know what early-to-bed evenings really mean, and they also know not to bother Mom and Dad when the bedroom door is locked in the middle of the afternoon.

❑ **The prudes.** These parental stiffs do everything necessary to avoid discussing sex with their kids. Usually prudes are the parents you think don't have sexual intercourse unless they're attempting to procreate. And usually, these parents have no trouble procreating either. Sadly, the prudes talk to their kids about sex only when something bad has happened and it's already too late.

❑ **The self-righteous.** These are holier-than-thou mums and pops with a fetish for guilt-ridden lectures. They are usually quite handy in delivering a good dose of antimasturbatory doctrine, too. The self-righteous parents don't simply teach virginity; they generate it. *Nothing* gets by these sharp-eyed, tongue-lashing folk.

❑ **The best friends.** Every kid has a friend whose parents are like the coolest of all parents. The "best friend" parents don't talk about sex with their kids; they would rather allow their kids to explore it all for themselves. Despite their churchgoing ways, they believe that to interrupt love would be to interrupt nature. Consequently, the best friends many times end up being grandparents a little before their time.

❑ **The just rights.** Most kids want to hear about intercourse from their parents no more than two times, and the just right mothers and fathers are okay with that! Giving their children just enough sex information to get by, the just rights share little "how to" and instead are more into the facts about sex. Despite not knowing everything about the ins and outs, their kids usually end up learning the trade by trial and error and trial and guilt and then error again. And *then* another trial.

After thinking through all the information I had gathered from my friends, I realized the world needed another book about sex. Before that, I wasn't sure a new book was needed. But that changed when I heard my friends' stories and thought through my own. I realized that Christians, young and old, married and single, need to begin talking healthily about sex. We need a book that will help us get that conversation started. We need a book that talks frankly about sex and the problems we encounter. We need one that will not make us feel all alone in the struggle.

Sexual Healing Exercise for Christians

Repeat this sentence:
It's okay for me to talk about sex.
Say it again, but this time, say it with lots of feeling, as if your tenth-grade theatrical teacher were asking you to recite it in front of the school's assembly.
It's **OKAY** for me to talk ABOUT **SEX**.
Very good! Now, scream it at the top of your lungs.
IT'S OKAY FOR ME TO TALK ABOUT SEX!
Now, one last time, and this might be a bit tricky for some of you. But I think you'll do fine; my confidence in your sexual healing is on the rise. Please, say the phrase with me in Spanish!

Está bien para mí hablar acerca del sexo.

Good job. Isn't it healing to be able to say those words out loud? I bet you're already beginning to feel this book's healing powers. If not, do not worry your sexually frustrated head. The transformation process will begin soon enough.

Basically, we need a book that will help teach us the things our parents didn't, or couldn't, for the sake of all of us.

Four Types of Responders to This Book

Responses to this book will vary greatly depending on your current sexual outlook, sexual history, theological stance, and whether or not you've ever gotten aroused while reading the book of Song of Solomon. But if my Christian wits serve me even moderately well, I believe most of you will have one of these four responses:

1 **The love-of-a-good-adventure type.** This individual will find the topics covered in this book delightful, lining up with near perfection to his or her own adventurous feelings about Christian sexuality. Moments of exceeding great joy are likely. Although some of the book's borderline *cheesy*

descriptions might cause sporadic bouts of nausea, ultimately the felt companionship he or she feels with the book's refreshing expressive candor will win out.

2 **The agreeable-yet-still-hesitant type.** Because this individual has a close relationship to the topics covered, he or she will laugh and nod knowingly throughout this book. Despite moments of boisterous unfettered glee, mild attacks of guiltlike sensations will occur. Still battling occasional fundamentalist urges, this person will have a subtle apprehension toward the book's honest approach that will teeter between absolute pleasure and hyperventilation.

3 **The mean-spirited-Amazon.com-reviewer type.** Appalled that a Christian book would discuss honestly the tension between faith and sexuality, this individual will passionately throw my little book back on the Borders' bookshelf after having read only three of its pages. A reddish hue will form on brow, across cheeks, and around neck. And in an effort to bring spiritual warfare against the book's content, this individual's only viable retribution will be to proclaim his or her angst on Amazon.com by giving the book a one-star review. Of course, expect this individual to make clear in the review that he or she would have rated the book "no stars" if that option had been available.

4 **The righteous-fan type.** This individual is apt to become one of the book's biggest proponents; she will talk to friends about it, blog about it, join the fan club, and spread the book's good tidings to all who will listen. Commonly referred to as wife of book's author, the righteous fan will ensure every one of her frequented bookstores carries the book. In an effort to

bring greater notoriety to author, she performs covert operations where book gets replaced from correct spot in bookstore to prime viewing spot. Said fan is also a great lover.

Growing Up Christian, Learning About Sex

[the thrill of knowing and the agony of being taught]

> The best sex education for kids is when Daddy pats Mommy on the fanny when he comes home from work.
>
> — William H. Masters

Your Sexual History

Let's begin this first chapter with a question. It's a little personal, but not too bad . . . yet. Here goes . . .

Have you ever thought about your sexual history?

I believe this is a very important question. Perhaps it's an unsettling inquiry for a few of you, but it's certainly one that's worthy of at least a little bit of your serious contemplation. However, I know that not all of you are taking this question seriously. A few of you don't believe the question is for you; so right now as you're reading these words, instead of contemplation being written on your face, a huge grin sits there, one that reeks of a strange mixture of cocksure and innocence. "I'm a virgin, Matthew," you'd say to me if you and I were in conversation with each other. "Yep, I've got absolutely no sexual history. NONE! I'm still 'untouched.' This isn't relevant for me. Is it okay if I just skip to the next section?"

Not so fast.

>>**I have to admit something here.** I am always a little freaked out by the way Christians advertise their virginity. Don't get me wrong, I am pro virginity before marriage; I think that's God's ideal plan. But I'm not so sure he ever intended our chaste behavior to be something that we flaunt like an ugly dude flaunts a hot date. I've had some of the strangest meetings with virgins. "I'm a virgin," they'll say to me. Okay!?! I'm

not sure if they're simply making a statement, repenting, or if there's a secret "please help me" message that I am supposed to pick up on. Sometimes they say it in a tone that suggests they're expecting God, at any moment, to ignore the poor people, the wars, and, not to mention, those who are still clueless about his plan for redemption, and hand them a big old trophy that reads, "I am proud of this virgin!" Talking virginity is especially awkward when it's with a virgin who is over the age of thirty-five. And please know there is NOTHING wrong with being a virgin over the age of thirty-five. In fact, it's EXTREMELY admirable. But does it have to become your personal tagline? Like, "Hi, I'm Jenny; I'm thirty-six years old. I like horseback riding; I'm a nurse. And you might like to know, I'm still a virgin!" I think this is weird. **Okay, back to your regularly scheduled content. <<**

As I was saying before the smaller font interrupted me, don't skip to the next section so quickly. I've got news for those of you "untouched" folk; your sexual history is about a lot more than whether or not you've had any official "play." So before you pull out your chastity belt and flash it my way, give me a couple of paragraphs, and I'll explain where I'm going with all of this.

Those of you who *have* had a little play, whether it's full-on play, limited play, or guilty feelings about solo play, are probably not convinced either that you should have to answer such a peculiar question, at least not honestly. You probably think I've gone and gotten all Dr. Phil on you. And you might actually be on to something. But come on, unlike Dr. Phil,

I CAN MAKE A STATEMENT WITHOUT USING EVERY EXPRESSIVE MUSCLE ON MY FACE.

And I can do it without hollering, too.

Truth to Know

It takes wisdom to build a house,
and understanding to set it on a
firm foundation;
It takes knowledge to furnish its rooms
with fine furniture and beautiful
draperies.
It's better to be wise than strong;
intelligence outranks muscle any day.
Strategic planning is the key to warfare;
to win, you need a lot of good
counsel.

(Proverbs 24:3-6)

So before you verbally open up and share all of your sexual history, let me explain exactly what I mean by sexual history.

I believe an individual's sexual history is made up of much more than simply one's sexual track record. Your sexual history, although it certainly includes all of your actual sexual experiences, might also include realities such as these:

1. Your sexual education

How you learned [or, as the case might very well be, *didn't* learn] about sex definitely is a part of your sexual history, whether you learned the old-fashioned way—from your parents—or while standing in your underwear in the locker room.

2. Your good, bad, and ugly life experiences

Life experiences, whether they're good happenings, awful distresses, or ugly situations, affect one's sexual viewpoint. Anything from the divorce of your parents to one of your friends being the victim of sexual, physical, or mental abuse to your sister becoming pregnant outside of marriage to the mystery of falling in love to having an embarrassing moment regarding sex — and these only scratch the surface — can affect what and how you think about sexuality.

3. Your parents' relationship with each other

Your parents' relationship is quite influential, much more than you probably realize. It's certainly not difficult to understand; how you perceive the relationship of your parents — and certainly not just their sexual relationship but also their emotional and spiritual connection — can be something that affects your sexual history. And it's not just a negative relationship that can affect you. If your parents' relationship is healthy, that fact

Do You Know Where the Lips You're Kissing Have Been?

FACT: Before you go kissing your significant other, it might be wise to know this: Germs reside in saliva. *Eek!* A peck on the cheek or a kiss on the lips doesn't cause too much of a threat. But kissing *à la French* could bring you cold sores, flu, mono, strep, or meningococcemia! *And who wants to get meningococcemia?* I'm not sure what exactly that is, but by the sound of it, you might just want to hold hands until you're married.

can play a very positive role in your sexual past, too.

4. Your impression of God and his view of sex

A person's perspective of God, whether it is right, wrong, or slightly misguided, greatly affects not only the spiritual aspect of sex but also how an individual perceives the concept of his or her own sexual desire. How we view God's feelings toward sexuality and also his feelings toward us often shapes our perception about our sexual desire. Consider this: If you've ever thought that God's sole desire was to catch you [and then smite you for] thinking a sexual thought or having a sexual encounter, that's a part of your sexual history. And seriously, how many Christians haven't at least once or twice or 347 times had the *God is going to smite me* thought?

5. Your environment

If the environment you've grown up in has been hostile toward sex, or if your surroundings do nothing but sensationalize or abuse sex, these influences can alter your sexual perspective and, thus, should be included as a part of your sexual history. Think about it: An individual whose father kept a large collection of pornography under his bed has probably been affected, regardless of whether or not the kid looked at the porn. Or on the other end of the spectrum, an individual whose overly religious mom got angry every time a reference to sex was mentioned in her presence probably has been provoked to think about sex in light of that happening over and over again.

I'll get back to the "question" a little bit later.

Learning Sex

A person's sexual history, whether you're eighteen or thirty-five, greatly influences your current sexual outlook. For the majority of us, the most influential part of that sexual history is how we learn about sex. As I'm sure you know, being Christian can sometimes make life confusing. And little else muddles up the concoction of faith and human nature like sex. Perhaps that's why so many Christians act funny when talking about it. They're scared the truth might cause a chemical—or physical—reaction. So instead of talking about it, a Christian tends to keep his sex life [or lack of sex life] under lock and key. Sadly, that's a consequence of what and how we've been taught to think about sex.

QUESTION: Hi, Sex Book! I'm a sophomore at a Christian university in Virginia, and I was wondering if you could tell me why humans have pubic hair. — Jason, 20

ANSWER: Oh, my dear Jason, pubic hair is indeed one of those human mysteries many wonder about. However, we, "the editors," do have a couple of theories you can ponder. One common idea is that genital and under-the-arm hair locks in scents called pheromones. It is believed that, for some humans, these "scents" can increase sexual desire. For others, they simply *stink*. Others have thought pubic hair is for warmth, some have said it's simply a little "color" to bring attention to the genital region, and finally, there are those who believe it somehow protects the penis or vagina. But honestly, nobody *really* knows why God gave us short and curlies. Because their function is up for debate, many men and women shave, trim, or wax the pubic region. I know — too much information. Tootles for now . . . and big hugs,

>>The editors

PS: Write us! Our e-mail is WeLoveWritingForMatthew@ yahoo.com.

Harsh Teachings on Sex

Perhaps you're one of the many Christian kids whose parents were unnecessarily harsh in regard to sex. Some of you might even describe your parents' teaching style as borderline psychotic. Sadly, the harsh technique was — and is — more common than one might realize. Children raised in the eighties and early nineties especially were subject to fanatical legalism.

I knew a guy a few years back whose mom told him she believed he was acting "lascivious" around the girls at church. "I am *not* having a son of mine being guilty of lasciviousness," she'd say to him every time her perception of a situation warranted it. My friend's mother had no idea how her harsh words affected her son. First of all, who uses the word "lasciviousness"? And secondly, is it possible to take a person who uses the word "lasciviousness" on a regular basis seriously? My friend's outlook on sex was altered rather intensely; as a young college student, instead of heeding his mother's warning, he ended up spreading his lasciviousness all over town, with every girl who would let him.

Of course, my friend was responsible for his own actions. His mother certainly didn't make him sleep around. However, she did indeed play a role.

The "legalist" view of sex has hurt a lot of people. My friend's story is simply one of hundreds I have heard, read, or experienced over the years. After realizing the effects of this harsh form of "sex education"—a term I struggle with using for this particular methodology—I have realized that possibly the worst part of this sexual philosophy is that it makes one feel like he or she cannot or is not allowed to talk about sex. This might seem like a rather unimportant detail to you. But it's not; not talking about sex can be a *huge* problem. Harsh rules regarding sex often cripple an individual's ability to be honest about what's *really* going on in his life sexually. Consequently, when dealing with the ramifications of his past, which might include everything from an unsatisfied sex life inside marriage, uncontrollable addiction to pornography, sex with people he hardly knows, or all of the above, the person whose religious background is filled with legalism keeps his problems secret out of fear that his "issue" might ruin his Christian life. And if this person is *still* in a legalistic environment, truthfully, it probably would.

If you're not sure whether or not your parents used this method, please read through the checklist on page 39 and see if it jars any displaced, confusing thoughts about sex. If tears, anger, or a need to call your therapist ensues, your parents followed this method. If not, your parents were probably way too easy on you. [That's a joke.]

Other Ways We Learn About Sex

Certainly, conversations with our parents aren't the only ways Christians learn about sex. In fact, I was quite resourceful when desiring to learn about sex. From reading sex books at the library to asking my Bible teacher uncomfortable questions about David and Bathsheba to hearing about the "bad" kids' sexual mistakes, I learned it all. Well, I didn't know it all, probably didn't even know half of it, but I knew enough to pretend I knew it all.

As a Christian teenager and into my college years, I found that learning about sex was kind of like putting a puzzle together. I had to keep searching through all the puzzle pieces until I found all of the border pieces. Slowly, I connected one border piece at a time and began to create the outside of the picture, and then eventually, I filled it in. As I discovered bits of information, I kept adding to my puzzle. Of course, I was thirty by the time I finished the puzzle. But I was putting the puzzle together without a picture to guide me.

O To begin the sex conversation with your child, start by ensuring that the environment where your child will be living for the next ten years is cut off from all worldly distractions. Worldly distractions include but are not limited to her unsaved grandmother, Billy Graham, and Vaseline.

O For best results, begin conversation by telling your child that sex is wicked and results in damnation unless one is married. Tell her that when God made Adam and Eve, he performed a wedding ceremony right there in the garden, and then [and ONLY then] were they allowed to copulate.

O This might be a good time to mention that God made Adam and Eve, not Adam and Steve. Make sure she knows the difference.

O Tell your child that talking about sex might make her feel uncomfortable. Tell her those strange feelings are from the Holy Spirit.

O Now, talk to her a little about the events surrounding puberty. Start with this, "Child, you will soon develop hair down there." [As you say the words "down there," just glance in the general direction.] Parents, explain only what you feel is necessary.

O After discussing the changes to her body, talk about how her feelings will soon begin to change toward members of the opposite sex. Tell her these "new" feelings are not permitted to be fully natural until marriage.

O Tell your child that on Monday nights, husband inserts [direct eyes *down there*] into a wife's [direct eyes *down there* again]. Then explain that after one to twelve minutes of motion, something happens in which babies are sometimes made.

O Ask your child if she has any questions. If questions create strange feelings, look disappointedly at your child. This should make all questions go away.

O One more thing! Make sure you tell her that guilt is her friend.

Popular Ways Many Christians Learn About Sex

⊕ **The middle-school dirty joke.** Sometime during middle school, you probably heard a joke with a punch line you're not sure you *really* got. But to avoid utter *non*coolness, you laughed anyway. Then you researched the punch line in an encyclopedia. [If you're twenty-four years old or younger, you probably Googled it.] However, if you were a *really* good kid, you ratted out the kid who exposed you to such trash and sent his butt to detention. *Anything for a pure mind, right?*

⊕ **Older siblings.** To that former twelve-year-old inside of you, a part of you believed your older siblings knew everything there was to know about sex. So during late-night talks, your sisters and brothers would drop the beans on what they had "experienced." Sure, it wasn't much, but it was better than watching *Anne of Green Gables*—again.

⊕ **Locker room lies [also hap-pened at sleepovers].** Most of the time, those who "lie"—who tell outlandish stories about their "sexual" escapades—are the guys

You Know You're Naive When . . .

[the following is true]

. . . you think French kissing is simply two people touching tongues tip-to-tip.

. . . you find a small foam ear-plug in your brother's coat pocket and think he's hiding condoms.

. . . you ask your brother, in front of your mother, if he's ever masturbated.

. . . your best friend gets in trouble for "mooning," and you have to ask your mom what that is.

. . . your roommate asks if you want to check out his pornogra-phy collection, and you think it has something to do with model cars.

who have had armpit hair since they were ten or the girls who have huge breasts when they're thirteen. Of course, you probably weren't brave enough to challenge their exaggerations, so you listened intently and then made it your own story when "bragger" wasn't around.

⊕ **Soft-core porn.** It hardly mattered that the sex wasn't real; heck, it didn't matter that there were lots of squiggly lines running across the television screen due to your parents' refusal to purchase a Cinemax subscription. None of that stopped you from pretending to channel surf. Of course, it always took you a second or two to figure out that the squiggly-lined channel *wasn't* the one you were surfing for. Sure, you now picture sex a little blurry and very wavy, but boy, did you learn something.

⊕ **The youth pastor's sexual horror stories.** You probably learned something about sex while attending youth group. In an attempt to be relevant, there's always one instance where a youth pastor [male or female] "gets honest" with a room full of kids. Usually, he ends up admitting the lust he felt in his heart for one of his old flames. Of course, by the time he told you this, he had rectified his guilt by calling the old flame and tearfully apologizing. And in some strange way, the confession made you and your own flame break up.

⊕ **The back of the bus.** Whether it's the school bus or church bus, something almost always happens in the back of buses, even when everyone is Christian. I know, I know; it wasn't your fault. The bad kids made you jump in one of the five back seats of the bus and play truth or dare. But admit it; you liked it. Sinner.

Experimentation

Lots of churches, in the way they avoid or hammer their messages on sex, do a gross disservice to Christians. Instead of creating environments where young Christians can learn and talk about sex, churches, Christian schools, youth workers, and parachurch organizations do little more than make young Christians feel stifled or condemned.

This often makes the problems worse, especially when one has experienced sexual intimacy of any kind. This is probably a bit obvious, but a lot of Christians do indeed learn sex by doing it or coming close to doing it. In fact, the statistics on Christian teenagers' sexual activity are almost identical to that of non-Christians.[1] The only positive difference is that Christians tend to wait a little longer before they have their first sexual encounter.

Teen Stats on Sex

According to a report in *Group Magazine* in 2004, more than 50 percent of Christian and non-Christian teenagers have had sex by the time they reach their eighteenth birthday. However, the study points out that instead of finding bliss, these sexed teenagers discovered a lot of pain.

- Just less than 25 percent experienced some kind of abuse [includes pushing, shoving, name-calling, or worse] in their first sexual encounter.
- Fifty-three percent of girls and 35 percent of boys said they'd change something about their first sexual experience.
- Sixty-one percent of girls and 40 percent of boys said they wished they had waited to have sex.
- Twenty-seven percent of boys and 24 percent of girls said they wished they had lost their virginity to someone else.[2]

Now, Back to That Personal Question

I'm sure you're well aware that one's sexual history has its consequences. All of the events that have influenced our view of sex both positively and negatively *must* be included.

The five "sex history" areas I mentioned before [sexual education; the good, bad, and ugly life experiences; your parents' relationship with each other; your impression of God and his view of sex; and your environment] are not a complete listing, of course. But they certainly give you an idea of what to consider when answering my question. *Oh, yeah, don't forget to answer the question.* You know, the question many paragraphs back.

Some of you struggle with talking freely about sex. I know, you did show good potential in the repeat-after-me therapy we experienced together a few pages back, but even still, there's a big part of you that's still not sure talking about sex is approved behavior.

For those of you who enjoy being tight-lipped about sex, I offer you four elementary reasons it's good for Christians to talk about sex. [After you finish reading the first list, make sure you check out the unofficial reasons that follow.]

FOUR OFFICIAL REASONS
YOU SHOULD BE TALKING ABOUT SEX

4. It's normal. You're not abnormal for wanting to talk about sex. Unfortunately, we Christians have made sex this QUIET issue that's about as comfortable to talk about as a colonoscopy. Talking about sex shouldn't be SO complicated. It should be a topic much simpler to open up about and discuss in a Christian setting — your struggles and all.

3. It's informative. In other words, you might surprise yourself and actually learn something. How's that for novelty? You might very well walk right into a comfortable, engaging conversation about sex with a couple of youth pastors at your church and come away from the conversation having new knowledge about sex. Yes, I know the chances are slim that two youth pastors would know enough about sex to pass along knowledge to anyone, but if the person was really naive, like super naive, it might work like a charm. You'd be surprised, I bet.

2. It's healing. When Christians are in an environment in which they feel comfortable engaging in hard conversations about sexual struggles, past mistakes, or abusive situations, talking about it can bring the chance for healing. And, seriously, have you seen the latest statistics? There is some real need for sexual healing on a variety of issues in the church. Often sexual issues leave us feeling hopeless, and many times we resist talking to other people about our struggles. Most of the time it's because we fear that our stories will be rejected, judged, or made into a miniseries on CBS. I don't know which would be worse, my sexual privacy leaking out around the church or it being at the mercy of CBS.

1. It's accountability. Speaking of healing, if no one knows what's going on inside your head or how you're feeling about a particular situation, how do you expect anyone to offer help? If you have questions regarding sex or simply need to vent your frustrations about being celibate, find someone you trust and talk about your predicaments. At least if you're talking about it, there's a chance that someone will respond.

FOUR UNOFFICIAL REASONS YOU SHOULD BE TALKING ABOUT SEX

4. Christians will use terms like *vulnerable*, *edgy*, and *progressive* to describe *you*.

3. You might *avoid* authoring *The Purpose Driven Virgin*. [I just *know* that someone is working on this title. I'd bet money on it — like two dollars.]

2. It's rumored that Pat Robertson has *never* talked about sex.

1. You might discover your spouse likes a talker.

TALKING BONUS: Okay, so I'm not a big fan of online forums, but I know many who are. So I would feel slightly behind the times if I didn't offer that as at least worth considering when wanting to engage in the conversation. If you happen to live in an area where Christians are still quite shy about discussing sexual topics, you might try taking your discussion to an online Christian forum. Try visiting the forums at Crosswalk.com or RelevantMagazine.com, where conversations about sex are filled with a moderate dose of Christianese, can still get mildly heated from time to time, and once in a while get downright honest. A couple of times a year, you might actually feel at home.

I'm rather confident that now, after spending the last couple thousand words thinking about your sexual history, you should be able to think about it in a little more open-ended manner than before. But know this: Some of you might find your history includes other areas, ones much different from what I have included. If that's you, don't be afraid to make that part of your answer. If you feel it has affected your views or concepts about sex and sex-related topics, include it.

In the space provided or in your journal, write down the key happenings of your sexual history. Although not every situation might have affected your current sexual outlook, go ahead and write everything that might have been influential. You can cross it off later if you want to.

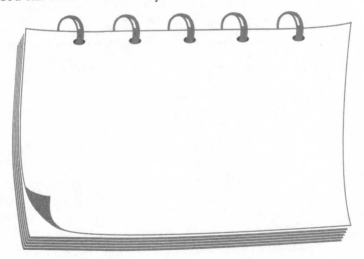

All of us tend to respond differently to situations. One might believe that masturbation has altered his perspective on sex; another might not consider it important enough to include. And a situation that is negative to one person might actually be positive to another. In all actuality, our sexual history can be rather confusing.

Okay, so if you're struggling with this "write down your answer" assignment, use the questions that begin to the right to help you get started. Basically, it's a self-interview. Except I thought of the questions, not you. If you want it to feel like a real interview, maybe you could ask your mother or sister or brother to ask these questions to you. I'm sure they would love to hear your answers. [*Yes, I'm kidding.*]

Thirteen Questions to Help You Identify the Key Elements of Your Sexual History

[Remember, these thirteen questions are only here to get you started. Of course, I could spend the rest of this book writing down questions that may or may not be relevant to you, and it STILL might not be complete.]

1 How healthy did you perceive your parents' married relationship to be? Would you compare it to Fred and Wilma? Fred and Barney? Fred and Dino? And also, when you were nine, did you perceive their relationship differently from when you were sixteen? If yes, how so?

2 How did you first learn about sex? Did your mother teach you? A teacher? Your seventh-grade boyfriend? Lil' Kim? Do you remember what you learned?

3 How did your pastor or youth pastor present his perspective of sex? Was it approached positively? Negatively? Angrily? In other words, which of these influential men did your pastor most emulate when he spoke about sex: Jerry Falwell, Rick Warren, Dr. Phil, Jay Leno, or Condoleeza Rice?

4 Has there been a time in your life where you were abused emotionally, mentally, physically, or sexually? If yes, write down a short explanation. Have you ever witnessed anyone else being abused?

5 When you think about God's view of sex, what are the first five words that come to mind?

6 What was your first pop-cultural experience with sex? In other words, when did you first realize that information about sex could be found through magazines, the Internet, TV, movies, music, and so on? What was your first reaction to your finding? Intrigue? Disgust? Fear?

7 Have you ever been ridiculed, made fun of, or humiliated because of something sexual?

8 As a child, did your parents encourage you to talk about sex, or were you forbidden to discuss it?

For some of us, this conversation is difficult. Many are not thrilled about digging into their "sexual" past. For some, it's just too personal; for others, it feels like a colonoscopy. *Shivers!* Then again, some are quite comfortable with it, but they're also the people who streak in public places. For many of us, talking about the intimate details of our lives is as easy as discussing natural gas.

I've been on both sides of the coin. Today, I'm rather comfortable talking about sex. However, I've had moments when talking about the "past" made me feel like I was in one of those dreams where you show up to work naked, and no matter how hard you try to make yourself go back and put clothes on, it's impossible.

Here's the deal: Your sexual history, whether you realize it or not, plays a major role in how you think about, experience, and struggle with sex today. Of course, if you've experienced only holy and healthy concepts of sexuality throughout your past, then you probably have no problems; in fact, you might be perfect. If that's you, write me an e-mail that says, "I'm PERFECT!" in the subject line, and I will send you a personal gift. I just love perfect people. And you'll like the gift!

But before you write that e-mail, read the next paragraph.

9 Have you looked at pornography? If so, has it turned into a habit? An addiction?

10 Have you ever experienced sexual contact with another human being? Was it a positive experience? In other words, how did it make you feel? [NOTE: Just because it's considered biblically immoral to have engaged in a sexual act before marriage, that doesn't mean it has to have been a negative experience. Just write down honestly how it made you feel.]

11 Do you have a positive opinion about your body?

12 When you think about getting married, what most excites you about sex? Have you ever felt fearful about sex within marriage?

13 What role has guilt played in your life?

The probability of your sexual past being absolutely perfect is about as good as Tom and Katie's chances of staying together forever. I think it's safe to say that all of us, in some way or another, need to work on thinking about sex in a more healthy and holy manner [you know, the whole point of this guidebook]. However, if you truly think you're perfect, and I know some of you do, write this down in your sexual history: *Help! I am narcissistic.* I know that's harsh. Okay, yes, it might very well be as harsh as the legalistic rules to a sex talk. And really, you're probably a super nice person, but [a really big *BUT*] a healthy dose of humility will do you and those who hang around you on a regular basis some good.

Overexplanation

Anytime a Christian writes about sex, it's an unwritten rule that you will have to do some major overexplaining. You can't leave anything up to the imagination. You remember the dangers of an untamed imagination, right? Yes, the one your youth pastor warned you about! Well, because of that, I am going to sit here and overexplain sexual history one more time. For those of you who don't need the overexplanation, this might be a good time to confess the sins of your imagination.

Okay, so as the title of this book says, we're discussing what you *DIDN'T* learn from your parents about sex. And the first order of sexual business in pursuing a healthy and holy sexual lifestyle [I mentioned healthy and holy in the introduction] is to know your sexual history. This is important for holy and healthy sexual living. I believe some of the problems, anxieties, fears, mistakes, and misconceptions Christians experience regarding sex and sex-related issues—in marriage and in the single life—often stem from a resistance to understand our sexual pasts in a healthy manner. If an individual hasn't learned how to manage her sexual history, whether that history was yesterday, six months ago, or twenty years ago, then it becomes much more difficult to manage and pursue good habits today.

Of course, I use the word *manage* like I'm a supervisor at the Gap, but for some reason the word seems to fit rather nicely.

Just remember, sexual history affects the way you view sexual desire. It gives you either a positive, healthy view of sex or a negative, tainted, addictive, or even fearful view of sex.

Here's one example of a poor history creating problems in a couple's marriage.

In preparation for this book, I interviewed a lot of people in their twenties and thirties, both married and single—all Christian. One young married woman, a twentysomething marketing specialist, wrote to me about the fear she felt when she first began experiencing an orgasm; she was literally frightened by the sensation of what she was feeling. "I told my husband to stop doing what he was doing," she wrote. "I know this sounds stupid, but the act of sex is hard for me to enjoy; it feels almost dirty." When I e-mailed her back and asked her

One Guy's Sexual History

Twenty-seven-year-old Kristofer is a graduate of UCLA. He's single. Kristofer says he's been following Jesus in some capacity since he was nine years old. He was one of several young adults I asked to write down their sexual history. After explaining what I meant by "sexual history" — for some reason I had to explain that every time — Kristofer's reflection of his past opened some pretty tough wounds. I interviewed him for this book:

MPT: When you finally took the time to write down your sexual history as this book defines it, what did you come up with?

KRISTOFER: [*Laughs*] A lot more than I would have thought was there. My folks never talked about sex at home. But that didn't stop me from exploring. My brother and I looked at porn a lot in high school. We just kept it hidden from Mom and Dad. In twelfth grade, I received oral sex from my girlfriend but felt really guilty afterward. [*Laughs*] I ended up confessing that to my youth pastor, which looking back I'm not sure was the right thing to do, because he ended up yelling at me and making me feel like I was about two inches tall.

MPT: Is that everything?

KRISTOFER: No. In college, I experimented with probably five or six girls. We didn't have sex; we just messed around. Every time something like that happened, I'd end up going through the routine of confessing to God; I'd cry and everything. But I'd always go back.

MPT: What are your experiences with sex today?

KRISTOFER: I love thinking about it. [*Nervous laughter*] I'm better than I was back in college, but I still look at porn a couple times a month. But I haven't dated in a long time, so it's been twelve months or more since I've fooled around with any girl.

MPT: What part of your sexual history do you think most affects you today?

KRISTOFER: Honestly, I'm still figuring that out. All of it does to some degree. But I think the biggest thing has been that my parents never talked to me about sex, so I never got a positive or healthy perspective regarding sex. Every interaction with sex that I have ever experienced has been negative. And to some extent, I knew that, but thinking about it all at once has made me realize that I've never thought about sex in the right way, never had the chance.

why she believes she responded this way, she wrote this: "When I got married eighteen months ago, I was a virgin, not out of love for God but because I was scared that I would get caught and that my reputation would be ruined. . . . I've visualized sex being wrong for so long that I just couldn't enjoy it with my husband. . . . I started counseling three weeks ago." She went on to share that she knew her fears were ridiculous, but because she had never dealt with how sex had been presented to her, her ability to be happy in bed with her husband was crippled. "It hurts my husband, too," she concluded. "I mean, he's so patient with me, but deep down I know he feels unloved."

Wow, that's a deep story. So deep that I almost didn't include it in this book. Hopefully, her predicament is not too common. But truthfully, no one knows for sure. As far as I can tell, no research exists. [If you're married and this story rings true in any way, please consider visiting a counselor so you can be free and happy in your sex life.]

See how your sexual history can affect how you think about sex? Before you can begin to understand what Scripture teaches about sex, you need to figure out what you've already learned and how it has affected your thinking today.

Your Parents Done Good If . . .
[not a complete list]

. . . they taught you how babies are *actually* made

༆

. . . they spoke to you about masturbation

༆

. . . they gave you the age-appropriate information regarding sex throughout your life

༆

. . . they created a home environment where conversations about sex were natural

༆

. . . they talked to you about STDs

༆

. . . they talked frankly about not letting anyone touch you inappropriately

༆

. . . they explained to you the opposite sex's body parts

༆

. . . they showed you in the Bible where God talks about sex and sex-related topics

༆

. . . they made sex sound amazing

༆

. . . they themselves had a good sex life and made sure you knew it

Adventures in Learning Sex— First-Time Lessons

I received my first "lesson" at age six. A cousin touched me. I did not understand what was happening to me; I felt dirty about it for a long time.

— Taylor, 30

I was in fifth grade when I got my first lesson about sex from looking at pornography.

— Matthew, 20

I learned about sex from everyone — my youth pastor, camp counselors, etc. I think I got a well-rounded perspective. It included implications as well as examples to learn from.

— Allie, 25

I was molested at an early age by an older girl. After that experience, I remember being very sexually aware. Later in life, I feared sex because of that event.

— Harry, 21

My mother gave me a bunch of books and instructed me to read them. She told me, "If you have any questions, you can ask me." I do believe there was a discussion later on, but the embarrassment has erased any memory of that chapter in my life.

— Diana, 19

My father wore nothing but a bathrobe when he talked to me about sex. I've been scarred for life. [*Laughs*]

— Daniel, 27

Believe me, I know it's sometimes quite difficult being a happy virgin. Sure, we put on our best and *purest* grins, but sometimes it's impossible to be content, peaceful, *happy* about our chaste lifestyle. Well, here's a week's worth of fun ideas to help your pursuit of all things pure feel a lot more fun. However, here's the bad news: After the seven days are up, you're on your own.

DAY ONE: Start a chain letter! You remember how much fun chain letters were as a kid. Well, why not start one of your own? *It will be great fun!* And the freedom and joy you'll feel knowing that you are causing great annoyance in the lives of thousands will certainly be enough for you to forget your "frustrated" state of mind.

DAY TWO: Shame a teddy bear. Take your least favorite teddy bear [any stuffed animal will work] and tell it to go sit in the corner. If it refuses to respect your wishes, pick it up and throw it in the corner! Teddy bears don't care. But if it does talk back at you, put it on its back all day long with its arms and legs raised. *That'll teach it!*

DAY THREE: Start a Bible study group for married Christians. Once all your oversexed friends arrive, lock the front door so they can't escape. Then torture them by reading the first six chapters of Leviticus and making them watch the 251 minutes of *Return of the King*. Then politely say, "That's it; I'll see you all here next week!" When they get home that night, you can be sure of one thing: You won't be the only one *not* getting any.

DAY FOUR: Declare today random-lunge day. Whether you're at work or at the mall or at church, everywhere you go, break out into random sets of lunges. Don't walk to get your morning cup of coffee, lunge there. If the pastor moves you to visit the altar, lunge all the way down the aisle. You'll feel great knowing that you're exercising your thighs and helping to improve balance. When your friends, coworkers, or fellow worshipers ask you what you're doing, get all excited and say, "Haven't you heard? It's random-lunge day!"

DAY FIVE: Spend the entire day stalking your celebrity crush. Whoever your celebrity crush is, make it your passion today to get as close to him or her as you can. Write e-mails, send letters, look up his manager's phone number. When his assistant picks up the call, tell her you *must meet with her client* because you're the virgin God created to make all of his dreams come true. Of course, don't try this one unless you're sane enough to stop after twenty-four hours.

Give Me a Good Foundation

[This heading is so much cooler if sung to the tune of Marky Mark's "Good Vibrations"]

In order for a person to have a good sexual outlook in the future [and believe me, it's a crucial possession, one your future spouse will greatly appreciate], it's of utmost importance to be sure you've contemplated your history. And through the journey of contemplation, you'll more than likely realize how your sexual foundation today has been shaped by what happened many years ago. As you probably know, it's imperative for Christians to construct all of their sexual ideas and truths on a holy and healthy foundation. And sometimes your history can make getting that foundation a wee bit shaky.

DAY SIX: Picket something meaningless today. Choose a pointless cause, be it the dishes your roommate leaves piled in the sink, the blue pleated pants your boss wears on Mondays and Thursdays, or anything Jennifer Love Hewitt. Make some signs, stand somewhere people will see you, and demand your voice be heard. *Neve Campbell might send you a thank-you card.*

DAY SEVEN: Visit a cheesy tourist trap and claim you're unable to escape its evil clutches. When the authorities come to take you home, run to the back of the gift shop and hold on for dear life to the antlers of the store's stuffed moose head. As the police try to coax you away from the moose, surrender peacefully, begin crying, and tell them that the little cactus plants and cowboy ceramics were just too enthralling to leave on your own. As you leave, *wave bye-bye to all of the collectible spoons.*

BONUS IDEAS: Because I'm such a nice guy, I am giving you five more ideas. But the game plan to make them happen is all on you.

- Become Joan Osborne's long-lost super fan for a day.

- Claim you're the love child of a famous televangelist.

- Purchase Edvard Munch's painting *The Scream* and hang it on the wall above your bed.

- Become a Scientologist for the day! Make Tom proud.

- Call in sick, but then go to work anyway.

Okay, let me break it down with another stupid analogy. Let's say you're building a new house. If you want your house to actually remain standing, and that, of course, is the point of having a house, then the most important ingredient for sturdiness is to ensure that you have a well-laid foundation and that it's on solid ground. Ah, that cliché is killing me; I know it must be killing you, too. It's too Joel Osteen, isn't it? I'll work on it if I ever write this book again.

For now, I am keeping it, so work with me.

So, in light of my overused little house analogy, it's pretty obvious that a Christian would want to take some time to think about the current status of his *sexual* foundation. In other words, what do you currently build your sexual ideals upon? Is it your experiences? Your feelings? Your desire to be holy? What does your foundation consist of? This is intense stuff, huh?

Let me start with the good news! [On a side note, do any of you remember the Sunday school song that went like this: *Good news, good news, Christ died for me. Good news, good news, that I believe*? I'm actually singing it while I'm typing. It's a shame you can't hear me.]

Okay, back to the topic.

When it comes to a sexual foundation, there is no such thing as the ideal sexual foundation. Of course, this is where my "house" analogy gets a little shaky. Unlike when you build a house, there are no experts who can come into your life and assess where your values, experiences, or environment might be shaky. Sure, we can point to certain things in the Bible and learn a great deal about God's design of sex, but let's face it, many people interpret Scripture differently. What's sin for one person might be fine for the other. [We'll talk about the Bible and sex in the second section.] Fortunately for slightly messed-up people like us, there isn't a foundational checklist to determine whether or not we pass the "foundation" test. But before you get all excited about the fact that there's not a pass or fail scale in this book, you might want to know that there is, indeed, a "needs improvement" for all of us.

That's making you feel a lot better, huh?

Because of a various array of life situations, many of us have formed rather destructive ideas about sex, intimacy, and love. Some of these situations might include bad or harsh theology, dishonesty about our sexual struggles, sexual abuse or harassment, watching our parents' relationship fall apart, our own sexual activity, pop culture's definition of sex, or perhaps, worst of all, naiveté. These events, mistakes, and realities all play a major role in how we create our personal sexual foundation.

Like I said before, a Christian's spiritual calling is to live a lifestyle that is both healthy and holy [which, I should remind you, is indeed a lifestyle that includes the potential for *mind-blowing* sex within a marriage relationship]. But in order to pursue the sex life God designed for his followers, sometimes we have to backtrack a little. Sometimes before we're able to move forward in freedom, grace, and purity, we have to assess our foundation. When a Christian decides to reassess the values, experiences, and environment that make up her sexual foundation [Holy Rollers, I'm talking to you, too], this almost always brings to the surface a problem in the way we sexually think, believe, or live.

So hold on to that sexual history list you wrote down. We'll take another quick look at it in section 5. And I promise I am not going to make you burn it, cut it up, or nail it to a makeshift cross. *I promise.* But you will need it for the last section. So don't go ripping it out of the book. This book hates to be ripped.

Okay, so are you ready to make like Rocky and Bullwinkle and travel back in time to find out as much as we can about sexual truth as talked about in the Bible? It will be fun. I promise. Well, I guess it could be lame, but will you try to make it fun?

Try really hard.

The Bible and Sex

[what God's Word says about sexuality]

Sex is God's joke on
human beings.

— Bette Davis*

---

*Ms. Davis was not a Christian, but these words are still funny and often feel true — but
they're not.

First, before you begin reading this second section, I just have to say you were such a good reader on that first section. Of course, I'm aware that my writing tends to hover around a fourth or fifth grade reading level. But really, if this book read like a Dickens novel, would you have gotten this far? See? I make a great point, don't I?

So go ahead and give yourself a round of applause for making it through to the second section. Some of you might find it fun to resurrect that stupid thing you did as a kid when a teacher or youth pastor asked you to offer a round of applause. You know, you'd clap *really* loud and then spin your hands around in a circular motion. *I hated when kids did that.* Of course, I joined them once in a while, but that was only because I was insecure and needed friends.

Okay, stop applauding.

I don't want you to get prideful. I don't believe there's anything scarier than mixing sexual frustration with pride.

Let's get started on learning what you need to know about the Bible [as it relates to sex]. Are you excited? You're going to be so biblical when we're finished with this section. And you'll be pleased to know that it's very simple. Here's everything you need to know:

Point #1: **ONLY MARRIED PEOPLE CAN HAVE SEX!** [Yes, I'm yelling.]

Point #2: Don't have sex until you're married. [Of course, you might be forty and still not having sex. Hope you're good at waiting!]

Point #3: GET MARRIED!

Point #4: Have some of the worst sex ever because of a sheer lack of experience! [And love every minute of it.]

That's all you need to know! You're officially a biblical expert.

I'm kidding.

There are hundreds of things you can learn about sex from the Bible. Well, I say hundreds, but there might be thousands of things to learn, or there might be only twelve or so. It all depends on if you're conservative like Baptists or more open-minded like Episcopalians.

Sometimes the Bible reads as dry as the dictionary when talking about sex. Consider Leviticus with its directly stated rules about everything from not sleeping with one's mom to a woman's period being an inappropriate time for sexual intercourse. These verses get to the point. They don't hide their meaning in stories or with theology; they state God's feelings loud and clear and sometimes awkwardly.

Sometimes the Bible reads as juicy and blushing as erotica. What I love about the Bible is that it doesn't hold anything back. It's descriptive in its story, and if you can work past some of the strange and precarious language, you read about God's passion, emotion, and love of sex.

But sometimes, the Bible's "sex-related" stories are just strange. Consider the time when David killed two hundred men during one of his many battles. When he returned from war, he presented King Saul with all of the dead enemies' foreskins. *Huh?* Can you imagine getting a bag full of two hundred foreskins? But David's time on earth had several strange sexual happenings. Once when God got angry with David, he gave David's wives over to his neighbor [who ended up being David's son Absalom] and made sure he had sex with all of them in the light of day [and in front of the entire city of Israel]. *Sometimes I don't understand God.* [If you're struggling to believe this is in

I know of no greater failure among Christians than in presenting a persuasive approach to sexuality. Outside the church, people think of God as the great spoilsport of human sexuality, not its inventor.

— Philip Yancey, *Rumors*

the Bible, read 2 Samuel 12:11-12 and then 2 Samuel 16:21-22. I was shocked, too.]

Of course, within this section, I can't cover everything sexual from the Bible. *There's too much!*

But for your own sexual well-being [and for those around you], not to mention for the sake of your children and hopefully your spouse, too, I have conveniently compressed most of the important stuff you need to know about the Bible and sex into this one section of bite-sized literary bits. I've included everything remotely interesting or relevant or funny. However, I didn't think you'd need to be told that having sex with animals [otherwise known as bestiality] is an abomination [means disturbing, gross, worthy of smiting] unto God. If my assumption is incorrect, this might be a good time to put the book down and pray. Because I can't help you, nor do I really care to try.

[Insert awkward silence here — yours *and* mine]

Okay, let's get on with section 2. I have a hunch this section is going to be good. I can just feel it. However, I went to see *The Dukes of Hazzard* on opening day because I thought it was going to be good, too. I know, too much information. And what in the world was I thinking?

Let's learn something.

Five C-Words to Remember When Studying Sex in the Bible

[I love alliteration, except in sermons]

1. Context. Sometimes the Bible demands that we look deeper into God's truth and how it relates to us today. [However, between you and me, sometimes I don't think it's meant to make sense. Like God making David's wives sleep with his son—that makes no sense.] But don't settle for what a preacher or author says; it's good to take the time to educate yourself on why certain verses say what they do. By digging deeper—learning the history, knowing the meaning, and understanding why God said it in the first place—your faith and understanding might be strengthened by what you learn.

2. Culture. How is the verse, biblical story, or commentary affected by the culture in which it was said? How different was the culture during biblical times compared to what it's like today? Understanding the Bible's culture—which includes everything from customs to language, from habits to worldviews—will help you know not only what God expects but also why.

3. Community. Don't search for the answers alone. Engage the process of knowing God's perspective of sexuality by talking about it with friends, a pastor, or others who might be able to shed light on an area you don't understand. Every person should have a close group of people they feel comfortable enough around to discuss the hard issues. Remember, it's okay to ask questions. And, yes, when it's all said and done, you might have your own opinion. But don't form an opinion without working at it first.

4. Compare. Don't settle for one person's perspective. Compare Bible translations. How is the wording different? Do they seem to mean the same thing? Refer to different books on the topic. Exploring God's idea for sex requires that we engage in the process of learning and understanding as much as we can about his ideal.

5. Contemplate. When you learn something new or are reminded again of God's truth regarding sexuality, consider how it can be applied to your own life. Pray, ask for help, and then pursue an understanding of how your sexual lifestyle can be changed, bettered, freed up by wisdom and the grace of God's Word.

Stuff You Should Know ➠ God Made You a Sexual Being

All of us, even those of you who are called to the priesthood, are aware that sexual desire is an extremely powerful force living, breathing, and sometimes twitching inside of you. You did know the urges were normal, right? Well, if not, I'll say this for now: Sex can make a person do some crazy stuff. I can't tell you how many stupid life occurrences I have successfully managed to blame on the extremely powerful force of my sexual desire.

I mention this to remind us that this powerful drive — you know, the one that keeps a lot of us up at night, wreaks havoc on our relationships, and perhaps makes some of us do things we later regret—was indeed programmed into our personal DNA by God.

Yes, *by God*. I know it seems a little ironic, but it's true. Sex was invented/designed/created/perfected by God himself. In other words, he made it.

And I'm certainly happy he did. BUT . . .

I have to admit the whole God-made-me-a-sexual-human-being concept has, at times, been difficult for me to grasp. In all honesty, for most of my life [at least until recently], sex was a weird idea to think about.

Since I was five, I have always been fascinated with birds. While other boys played with their Atari or Tonka trucks, one of my favorite toys was a plastic eagle that had flappable wings. I also LOVED my Hawk Man action figure [Hawk Man was a superhero who could fly using his "hawk" wings]. I don't know why I loved birds so much; perhaps it's because I always wanted the ability to fly.

Anyway, when I was fourteen, my spring and summer job was at a marina on the Chesapeake Bay; I was a dock boy. Several ducks made their home at this marina. During my free time, I loved watching the ten or so mallard ducks that resided there; they waddled around, dove into the water to get food, and seemingly talked [or quacked] to each other constantly. *Okay, so I thought they were cute. Is that really such a big deal?*

But it gets worse.

Over the course of a couple of months, I felt like those ducks became my friends. Well, not my friends necessarily, but I felt like they knew me. One afternoon, a couple of them were swimming around, having a good time. All of a sudden a male duck jumped onto one of the female duck's back. He began jumping up and down on her head, pushing almost her entire body into the water. I watched in horror. It was one of the most violent scenes I had ever witnessed. *He's trying to kill her,* I thought. *I have to save her.* At first, I tried shouting at the male duck. He either didn't hear me or he was having too much fun playing massacre on my duck friend's back. He had to be the meanest of all the ducks; he just kept attacking her, despite her trying her best to get away.

I ran to the marina's storage closet and got a broom. Once I returned, I began beating the male duck off the female duck's

You think we live in an oversexualized world? Well, you're right; we do. However, you might be surprised just how much sex was going on — good and bad — during the time of Genesis. Some of the strangest sexual occurrences happened in the Bible — a lot of them right at the beginning. Here's a quick recap for those of you who aren't too savvy at Old Testament history:

◎ Adam knew Eve and then she conceived (see 4:1). *[That one rhymes!]*

◎ Cain knew his wife and she conceived, too (see 4:17). *[Of course, we aren't sure where his wife came from, and all of the possible answers somewhat frighten us . . . so we simply trust that God knew what he was doing.]*

◎ Adam knew Eve again and she conceived yet again (see 4:25). *[Poor Eve! Can you imagine how many times she had to know and conceive in her nine-hundred-plus years on earth?]*

◎ After the Flood, Noah got drunk and hung out in his tent naked. His son, Ham, which is a rather unfortunate name for a Jewish kid, saw him. Noah decided to curse Ham's son Canaan (see 9:18-25). *[Seeing people naked was a really big deal back then. I don't think Noah would have liked going to the gym.]*

◎ Pharaoh gave in to temptation and took Sarah, Abraham's wife, into his harem (see 12:15). *[Of course, God was ticked with Abraham over this because he had lied and said that Sarah was his sister. Sadly, God plagued Pharaoh's entire house! It must have sucked being a pharaoh — plagues aren't fun.]*

◎ Two angels visited Lot, and the Sodomites were sexually attracted to them (see 19:1-5). *[Lusting after angels is a recipe for utter destruction!]*

◎ God destroyed the cities of Sodom and Gomorrah (see 19:24-25). *[If this historic event hadn't occurred, what would preachers have to get upset about? I mean, would they all be home watching reruns of Will & Grace?]*

◎ Lot got drunk. His two daughters had sex with him and each became pregnant (see 19:30-38). *[Can you imagine THIS Bible story retold with paper dolls and a felt board? This has to be why I don't meet too many people named Lot.]*

- Regarding Rebekah, Isaac's wife, the Bible says this: "And the damsel was very fair to look upon, a virgin, neither had any man known her" (24:16, KJV). [This is pretty much saying that Rebekah was not only hot, but she was also pure.]

- Jacob "went in unto" Leah; he was too drunk to know that it wasn't his girlfriend, Rachel (29:23,25, KJV). [I'm not sure drunk is the right word here; he must have been pretty much derailed to not know he was sticking his member into foreign soil.]

- A week later Jacob finally "went in also unto Rachel" (29:30, KJV). But he had to work seven more years. [I don't know about you, but I love "romantic" stories where the dude finally gets the girl of his dreams and her older, homelier sister, too.]

- Rachel bartered her husband's sexual favors for her sister's mandrakes (see 30:15-16). [They must have been really nice plants.]

- Dinah, daughter of Jacob, was sexually defiled (see 34:1-12). [It's unclear whether or not this is rape or sex outside of marriage. Most assume the latter.]

- Dinah's lover made amends with Jacob, her father, by agreeing to have all three thousand men of his city circumcised. Dinah married her defiler (see 34:13-31). [Circumcision when you're a baby is one thing, but having it done so your buddy can marry his girl is quite another. Ouch.]

- Reuben, son of Jacob, slept with his father's concubine (see 35:22). [Yeah, this was a pretty devastating mistake; his dad told him he would not "excel" because of his evil actions (49:3-4, KJV).]

- Judah, another son of Jacob, married a Canaanite woman and "went in unto" her, and she bore a son (38:2-3, KJV). [Have you ever noticed that no one had daughters?]

- Potiphar's wife made sexual advances at Joseph; he fled (see 39:7-20). [However, Potiphar's wife lied and said that Joseph "came in unto" her (verse 14, KJV). He got thrown in prison for a very long time.]

back with the broom. That was no easy task. He was a tough little guy. But eventually, the male mallard flew off. And the little female duck swam back to the others.

When my father arrived to drive me home, I told him all about the ducks. "Dad, thank God I was there or that duck would have died," I said.

Dad started laughing. "Matt, that duck wasn't trying to kill her; they were mating. That's what ducks do."

"Mating?" I asked. "They were mating? But she didn't seem too happy."

"Well, I'm sure it wasn't all that pleasant for her, but that's exactly what was happening. That's how God made them," my father explained. "A lot of animal mating habits are a little different."

MATING HABITS? It was more like raping habits.

As my father and I drove home, I did a lot of thinking. And I pretty much concluded this: God's plan for procreating ducks is weird.

However, his plan for the procreating of humans is, at times, even weirder.

Perhaps I just think too much, but oftentimes it's been hard for me to imagine a God who is holy and grandiose and perfect creating something as odd as sex. It hasn't always seemed logical to think that God would create an act that requires two people to roll around naked in a bed together, screaming, kissing, sweating, and breathing heavily. And it doesn't stop there. On top of the nakedness and sweating, God designed this experience to conclude with an unbelievable [and hopefully mutual] spiritual, emotional, and physical event — the orgasm.

For a long time, trying to balance my limited and perhaps slightly tainted mental picture of sex with the holiness of God didn't seem possible. Sex seemed so human, while God seemed so otherworldly, so untouchable, so big. For me, sex didn't seem to be indicative of the God I knew, at least not the one I worshiped at my church on Sunday mornings. The God I knew seemed to be too stodgy to create such a desirable and engaging act.

But nonetheless, despite all of the issues, questions, and new ideas that arise concerning our sexual desires, he did indeed create us as sexual beings. When we read the first few chapters of Genesis, we capture the true picture of what God intended for human beings: nakedness without shame, procreation, pleasure, and prosperity. Sure, our humanness has messed with this plan along the way—I'll get to that soon enough—but take a moment and revel in the fact that you are sexually charged for a purpose. And that purpose is *good*.

Stuff You Should Know ⫸
God Created Sex For Procreation

I assume you know this one. You should know this one. If not, close this book and cry. You have reason to.

For those of you still reading, I have a couple of questions for you to consider.

When God told Adam and Eve to multiply [you know, to go *in unto* each other], did he explain the process to them? Did Adam look at God and ask, "Umm, God, when you say multiply, what exactly does that entail?" Did Adam just know what his penis was made for? Did Eve know why she had a vagina? Did they just know that the two do great things together?

Or did God, soon after he created them, spend time explaining the process of multiplying? If so, I wonder what that was like. Can you imagine learning about sex from God?

"Adam, I have bestowed upon you a penis and upon Eve a vagina. With these bodily items you will make babies. I think you'll like this procedure very much [insert a kind grin ☺ here]. I've thrown in a few added bonuses just because I can."

How much detail did God give? Did he let them in on what would happen when these two instruments come together? I'm assuming he didn't make them watch a DVD on the topic.

Obviously, despite the Bible not saying how the first humans learned about sex, somehow Adam and Eve did indeed learn that a male's sperm

Yes, This Is in the Bible.

When a man has a discharge from his genitals, the discharge is unclean. . . . When a man sleeps with a woman and has an emission of semen, both are to wash in water; they remain unclean until evening. (Leviticus 15:2,18)
We follow an awful lot of the Old Testament rules, so why not this one? Just a thought.

combined with a female's egg makes babies.* This function is CERTAINLY a big reason God made sex. However, whether the early followers of God knew any more than this is a biblical mystery, something I might have to ask God when he and I meet face-to-face.

Stuff You Should Know ▬▶ God Created Sex For Our Amusement, Bliss, and Enjoyment

Many Christian authors crazy enough to tackle a book about sexuality [yes, I consider myself a wee bit crazy for grappling with this topic] would be tempted to put a *but* after a statement like this one. Christians sometimes fear that without clarification, our words might be taken out of context or, worse yet, misunderstood. However, in many instances, though certainly not all, I believe clarification takes away from the bigness and importance of a statement such as this one.

I believe that before Christians hear the rules, the do nots, the junk some churchy people try to sell as truth, they need to first know that one of the reasons God created sex was for human enjoyment. Before we can pursue a holy and healthy sexual lifestyle, we have to hear and learn about God's sexual perspective.

---

* See sidebar on page 107 for a detailed explanation of how babies are made.

The Bible talks vividly about sex being something intended for enjoyment. Sure, it doesn't always read like a Kama Sutra book, but neither is it simply a rulebook. With both story and truth, God inspired the writers of the Bible to paint a dramatic, intense, and pleasurable picture of sexuality.

Truth to Know

Blessed be the God and Father of our Lord Jesus Christ, who has blessed us in Christ with every spiritual blessing in the heavenly places, just as he chose us in Christ before the foundation of the world to be holy and blameless before him in love. He destined us for adoption as his children through Jesus Christ, according to the good pleasure of his will, to the praise of his glorious grace that he freely bestowed on us in the Beloved.

(Ephesians 1:3-6, NRSV)

As I began to research the Bible, I noticed an ongoing characteristic regarding sexuality and its emergence in the biblical stories: It was seldom the focus of stories, but it certainly accented many of them. This trait makes researching sex within Scripture somewhat difficult. But I was indeed happy to find that the "pleasure points" are there.

In Genesis, when Isaac lied to a community about Rebekah being his wife [he said she was his sister], his lie was discovered when he was caught fondling [groping, playing with, Baptists might call it petting] his wife (see 26:8). *Regardless of what you call it, they were enjoying it.* Many theologians believe that when God said, "A man leaves his father and his mother and clings to his wife, and they become one flesh" (2:24, NRSV), he was speaking of the great sexual pleasure experienced, because procreation is not mentioned around the idea of becoming "one." Again in 3:16, when God was telling Eve the ramifications of her disobedience, many believe his comment was referring to sexual desire:

"I will greatly increase your pangs in childbearing;
    in pain you shall bring forth children,
yet your desire shall be for your husband." (NRSV)

Of course, Solomon's poetic words in his Song outstretch most other Old Testament sexual allusions. His description of sex is so visual that many times throughout history [mostly during the Middle Ages], religious people have wondered whether unmarried Christians should read it. Some argued—and a few still do—that a person should be thirty years of age before being allowed to obtain a copy of Solomon's book.[1] It's passages like this one that for centuries have been making young boys and girls think of a whole bunch of sexual innuendos:

He took me home with him for a festive meal,
    but his eyes feasted on *me*!

Oh! Give me something refreshing to eat—and quickly!
Apricots, raisins—anything. I'm about to faint
with love! (2:4-5)

*I do believe a meeting such as this one might end with a little mess
to clean up; apricots ARE juicy.*

Here's the bottom line: Sex isn't simply for making babies;
it's also for eroticism, sensuality, and utter physical expression.

[All together now]

THANK YOU, GOD.

The Story of Onan Is Not About Masturbation. Whew!

For as long as I can remember hearing about masturbation — I am, of course, part of the 5 percent of men who have *never* done such an act* — I have known someone who quotes the story of Onan as biblical proof that God indeed killed a man for masturbating. I think it's time the TRUE story was told. Here it is; my handy in-depth commentary is found below:

> So Judah ① told Onan ②, "Go and sleep ③ with your brother's widow; it's the duty of a brother-in-law to keep your brother's line ④ alive." But Onan knew that the child wouldn't be his ⑤, so whenever ⑥ he slept with his brother's widow he spilled ⑦ his semen on the ground so he wouldn't produce a child for his brother. GOD was much offended by what he did and also took his life. ⑧ (Genesis 38:8-10)

① Judah was one of the sons of Jacob [you know, the guy who wrestled God] and a brother of Joseph [yes, the same guy who became second-in-command of all of Egypt].

② Judah had two sons: Er and Onan. Judah found a wife for his son Er. But apparently, Er sucked as a human being, and because of that, God took him out.

③ This was a very strange law that was enforced among those who were part of the tribe of Levi. Being made to sleep with your dead brother's wife might be a little awkward for anyone.

④ A bloodline was extremely important during early Jewish times.

⑤ Impregnating his brother's wife didn't interest Onan.

⑥ Looks like he might have done this more than once.

⑦ Basically, this means that during intercourse with his brother's wife, Onan pulled his penis out and ejaculated onto the ground.

⑧ Moral of this story: If you're part of the tribe of Levi and your brother dies, don't ejaculate onto the ground when you've been asked to impregnate your sibling's widow. That's a fine lesson indeed!

So here's the truth: Onan wasn't masturbating! In other words, masturbation is never mentioned in the Bible. *You are now free to jump up and down if you would like.* Of course, I'll be talking more about this in section 3, and some of you will have to stop jumping because it ends up being a little more complicated than this.

ONE OTHER NOTE: It might also be worth mentioning that some churches [mainly Catholic] use this story as a case against birth control.

---

* *Yep, I'm lying.*

Stuff You Should Know ➠
Holy Sex Should Be REALLY *Hot* Sex

Okay, I'm going to get on a soapbox for a moment.

I find it rather nauseating how some Christians talk about sex. A few years ago, I had the "distinct honor" of interviewing a Christian sex therapist. *[Does anyone else think Christian, sex, and therapist is a strange combination of words?]*

One of the five questions I asked my distinguished guest was this one: "Doctor, can you talk about what you believe a good sex life should entail?"

He looked at me seriously, took a sip of his coffee, and said this: "That's a good question, Matthew! I firmly believe that sex should be a joyful and peaceful experience between you and your spouse. It should be as a type of incense before God. He should smell it and be glorified. You do realize that sex was designed to be a beautiful reflection of God's love for his children, right? It's a very worshipful experience that a husband and wife are permitted to share sex—a pure language of love—within their bond of marriage."

When the doctor had finished his answer, I was left with a bit of frustration. I thought maybe the forty-year-old therapist had heard the wrong question. I thought perhaps that,

What You Didn't Learn from Your Parents About Sex Presents:
Answers to Your Most Intriguing Sex Questions!

QUESTION: What counts as losing your virginity?
— Becky, 30

ANSWER: This is a tricky question, Becky. I know we say that a lot. *So many* of the questions involving sex and sexuality are tricky [and sometimes rather sticky, too]. However, here's what we think: Loss of virginity *officially* occurs during penile/vaginal intercourse. During this type of intercourse, a man's penis breaks the hymen, which is a thin membrane of skin [*hymen* is Latin for membrane] that partially covers the opening of the vagina. [Clarification: But do know that a woman's hymen can be broken without engaging in intercourse. A tampon, masturbation, exercise, horseback riding, gymnastics, cheerleading, or a normal physical at the

right in the middle of this interview, which was all about sex, a sudden lapse of sanity had caused me to ask for his thoughts on singing praise-and-worship songs in church. I thought to myself, *This can't be his whole answer about sex.*

But he was serious. In fact, he even looked at me and said, "That sounds amazing, huh?"

I could hardly respond. So I just nodded awkwardly.

I sat there stunned. I was single and was suddenly wondering why the heck I was working so hard at waiting around for something that seemed about as exciting as PBS on Sunday afternoons.

That's how *a lot* of Christians view married sex—like

"a beautiful reflection of God's love for his children." Well, I have to say this: *Yuck!* I mean, yes, sex is a beautiful reflection of God's love for us, but come on! Do we have to talk about it like it's Presbyterian liturgy?

Speaking of sex like it's the equivalent of fellowship time in the church vestibule is rather limiting. It's no wonder it's so difficult embracing an exciting perspective of holy sexuality. I believe the word *holy* should represent everything good about sex. In fact, *good* hardly begins to describe how UNSTINKIN' BELIEVABLE holy sexual relations can/should/would be if we Christians unleashed the true meaning of the word *holy*. We often make the word *holy* a boring, loaded word used only in church and for people who act better than everyone else.

doctor can all be reasons the hymen becomes broken. None of these actions constitutes the loss of virginity.] When a male and female engage in penile/vaginal intercourse, they both lose their virginity. Outside of marriage, loss of virginity for both men and women can often be emotionally damaging and can leave a very lasting impression. Depending on your spiritual, emotional, and physical history, the greatest amount of pain and frustration can actually occur in the mind and heart rather than the body. However, it should be noted that loss of virginity is often more difficult for women because of the physical change that happens to her body. [This topic will be discussed a bit more in section 4.] We hope that answers your question!

True love waits and never deflates!

Tootles!

>>The editors

PS: Let us know your thoughts at WeLoveWritingForMatthew@yahoo.com.

Thankfully—despite *holy* being a great word to describe sex—most people don't actually use it as an adjective for their sex life. Let's face it: All of us would be a little wigged out if a friend were to *ever* say, "Dude, my sex life is frickin' holy, bro!"

That would be kind of strange. BUT . . .

Sex, in its purest and most honest form, is meant to be nothing less than magical, erotic, sensual—*holy*.

Holy sex is magnificent. It's electrifying. It's an oh, Oh, OH MY GOSH kind of sex that leaves you feeling unbelievable and completely *guilt-free* orgasmic pleasure. That's the kind of sex life married people should strive for. That's the kind of sex life God designed. All one has to do is think about the physical power of the orgasm and it's hard to miss God's innate desire to overwhelm us with human [but holy] pleasure.

Describing God's idea of married sex as anything less than complete ecstatic pleasure* between a husband and wife is

Size Mattered to Some in Bible Times, Too.

Yet she increased her whorings, remembering the days of her youth, when she played the whore in the land of Egypt and lusted after her paramours there, whose members were like those of donkeys, and whose emission was like that of stallions.

(Ezekiel 23:19-20, NRSV)

[This topic will be discussed again in section 4 — I know you're excited.]

---

* Results vary depending on performance.

a rather big mistake, I believe. Holy sex should be good. It should be fascinating. It's meant to fill us not just physically but emotionally, mentally, and spiritually.

No, I don't want people to start telling me how *holy* their sex life is, but I do think it's imperative for us to change our perspective on the word *holy* as it relates to sexuality. Remember, the sexual life God planned for humanity should lead us to orgasmic heights and not to guilt, frustration, boredom, and apathy.

Oh yeah, holy sex is *hot*, but it's also

⇒ Pure in heart, mind, and body.
⇒ Sacrificial. In other words, your spouse becomes the focus, not you.
⇒ Within a married relationship. You know this one.
⇒ A journey. Good sex doesn't just happen. It's learned, experienced, and revealed. [I'll talk more about this in sections 3 and 4.]

Stuff You Should Know ⟶ It Isn't Good For Man [and Woman] to Be Alone

God made this statement, not me. For a long time, much like I misunderstood sex, I didn't truly "get" my need for a woman and a woman's need for me. For some reason, the very thought of my needing a woman made me feel dependent.

I guess I should explain, though, that I certainly did understand part of my need for a woman — I'm like any normal guy — but I had hardly scratched the surface. However, now that I'm married, I'm on a journey toward understanding it, embracing it, and making it core in my everyday life. And my wife is on that same path.

Before marriage, every time I would hear a preacher or biblical teacher mention, "It isn't good for man to be alone," I couldn't help but think of those three words Tom told Renee in *Jerry Maguire*: "You complete me." Such a cheesy line, but boy, in 1996 when that movie first released, that line made me cry like a blubbering fool.

The words were sweet.

They were tender.

They seemed almost true.

But one day I realized they weren't true.

Man and woman don't complete each other; they were never meant to. But they do need each other.

I think when some people, both men and women, hear this God-statement, they tend to focus on the fact that God only mentioned man. This is a flawed perspective, I believe. Consider this: According to a seminary buddy of mine, several of his professors believe that in Hebrew, the word used for "man" in this statement is a sexless reference to "humanity," not to a masculine being. [Think mankind.] In Hebrew, the word used for "man" when referencing man and woman changes to one with masculine connotations. God's statement has implications for both men and women, even today. In these eight simple words, God captures the mystery of marriage, sexuality, and his ideal plan to perpetuate life, goodness, and passion on earth.

I may upset a few of you with this statement, but I'm going to say it anyway:

You **NEED** a helpmate!

In other words, it would seem that according to God's original plan in Genesis, a helpmate is hugely important, an essential part of God's plan for your life. Yes, I know *helpmate* is a rather old-fashioned word. But it's the best word to describe this girl-boy union that God finds so irresistibly perfect. [PLEASE NOTE: Some Jesus-followers are indeed called to celibacy, but to me, the celibacy calling does not contradict or negate God's original plan for the union of man and woman. It simply means that those who feel called to celibacy are called to something different, and that's okay.]

I know some of you think you're quite capable on your own, that you're completely perfect and at God's best without a guy or girl [husband or wife] in your life. However, God says you're not. He says it's not good for you to be alone.

BUT WAIT! Don't get frustrated just yet.

It's extremely important for us to recognize what God *didn't* say, too. He didn't suggest here that a guy sucks if he is not married. He didn't say a woman's a failure if she is not married. He didn't say a person should act like an idiot and date anyone and everyone possible until he remedies his "not married yet" problem. He didn't say that any combination of man and woman was divinely appointed. And he didn't say that simply being married to a great Christian person would instantly fill the need.

He said, "It's not good for you to be alone."

Here's a question: Do you live your life with this God-given need in mind?

Before you answer this question, think.

A lot of people within the Christian culture are tempted to try to pursue self-sufficiency. Whether married or single, young or old, we often pursue becoming fulfilled on our own. Some of us look for fulfillment in things such as hobbies, our career, education, friends, church, luxuries, unhealthy habits, pornography, random hook-ups, and other areas of human interest. It doesn't matter if they are good or bad; God didn't ordain any of these earthly things to aid us in becoming who we were meant to be. We, the culture, have deemed these things important and fulfilling; we've deemed them sufficient to complete us.

Sure, some of these things are indeed important. That's not my point. I know we need education, church community, and friends. These things bring enrichment, nourishment, and communion to our lives. But only a helpmate, within the context of marriage, can fulfill the need God described in this statement.

Of course, some of us believe that God provides self-sufficiency. But I believe the Bible shares several areas in life that God cannot or chooses not to fulfill. *Yes, God can do everything and anything.* But consider this: When God made the first human being [Adam, of course], he could have looked at him and said, "I am always going to be enough for you. I am going to fill every need you will ever dream about. I am sufficient for your time on earth." But he didn't say that; for some God-reason he chose not to and instead chose to bring man and woman together to fill a human, God-designed need. That was his plan—to make part of himself become manifested through the union of man and woman.

Unfortunately, human logic, based on some pretty convincing arguments and experiences, has seeped into our culture's belief system. This logic leads us to think:

➤➤ Relationships get in the way of being all I'm meant to be.
➤➤ I don't want to think about dating until I'm out of college.
➤➤ I can't handle the temptation right now.
➤➤ People who get married at twenty are losers or from the South.
➤➤ Marriage stops you from becoming who you're meant to be.
➤➤ I want to live my own life before I settle down.
➤➤ Jesus is my boyfriend right now [he's all I will ever need].
➤➤ I can be absent within my marriage and still make it work.

I include this particular truth in this book because any of this thinking can directly or indirectly affect your sexual lifestyle. If we're not actively pursuing life with this need in mind, this need still gets filled, but in an unhealthy [and usually unholy] manner. Some of us look to pornography. Some of us jump in and out of relationships. Some of us fill it with work. Some of us have random hook-ups. Some of us are addicted to masturbation. Some of us are engaging in "online sexships." You might not know this, but within your actions, somewhere in this thing you call life, you're trying to fill this need. And honestly, some of us are quite creative in this area and have made ourselves believe we're completely fulfilled.

It's my hope that this will encourage and validate those of you who long to be married or are experiencing a serious relationship—your need is real. Of course, I don't think unhealthy dating habits are cool. And some people [myself included] have done a lot of stupid things in pursuit of being married. But I want you to know that thinking about and desiring marriage at nineteen is not ALL bad.

Some of us have a huge desire to be married and hate being in a predicament where we've seemingly been called to temporary celibacy until the right person comes along. Let's face it: In a lot of ways, this sucks. Consider a thirtysomething woman who has a very real desire for a married relationship. How is she to think? Sadly, many Christians will say to a person in this predicament, "God wants you to be content with the fact that you're single before he's going to put a man in your life. He's not going to give you something when you're not okay with where he's put you."

Umm, okay, I have a problem with this type of thinking. I am well aware that God wants us to be content in everything; however, I don't believe this means that we're required to become satisfied in our singleness before he will provide a helpmate or allow us to find the love of our lives. You'll go crazy thinking like that! And also, it's certainly possible to pursue being content and still really, really want to get married. In fact, I highly recommend it. Just learn to have a little grace with yourself; God does.

Now, for those of you who tend to resist thinking about this need or try to bury it or fill it with other stuff, I'm hoping this section will help you take a moment to refocus the way you view this God-instilled necessity in your life. It's important that we ask God to allow us to feel this need in a way that he would desire us to.

Nearly every day, my wife and I look at each other and say, "I need you." This might sound rather simple to you [or make you a little sick to your stomach], but when we say these words, we are acknowledging that together we are stronger. This is true in every aspect of life, which of course includes our sex life.

To God, the union of man and woman is of utmost importance; it's his design. God doesn't view marriage as the end of independence or freedom or as "settling down." In fact, he believes it to be just the opposite. I think God views marriage as another step toward fulfilling his dreams for you.

Okay, that part *was* a little Dr. Phil.

You don't need to know this, but it makes a good conversation piece ▶ Song of Solomon mentions breasts a lot.

Sure, this information isn't exactly the most important of sexual fare. But if you're a human living on planet Earth, you know that men, especially men in the Western Hemisphere, tend to go gaga for breasts. Well, guys, the Bible talks a lot about this desire; Solomon, yes, *King Solomon*, had an open affection for breasts, too. And any guy who gets inspired by God to poetically describe his wife's bosom as a "cluster of dates" has to be a pretty likable fellow. And what *amazing* breasts they must have been! Whether he was "petting gazelles" or "fondling fruit," when it came to his favorite things, Solomon didn't mince words.

I'm pretty sure we would have been friends. The following are King Solomon's words about breasts:

His head resting between my breasts.
(Song of Solomon 1:13)

Your breasts are like fawns,
    twins of a gazelle, grazing among the first spring
    flowers. (4:5)

Your breasts are like fawns,
    twins of a gazelle. (7:3)

You are tall and supple, like the palm tree,
    and your full breasts are like sweet clusters of
    dates. (7:7)

I say, "I'm going to climb that palm tree!
    I'm going to caress its fruit!"
Oh yes! Your breasts
    will be clusters of sweet fruit to me,
Your breath clean and cool like fresh mint. (7:8)

And then Solomon's lover makes this statement:

Dear brothers, I'm a walled-in virgin still,
    but my breasts are full—

And when my lover sees me,
>   he knows he'll soon be satisfied. (8:10)

Stuff You Should Know ⅢⅢ➡
Purity Is a Lifetime Calling
[Not Just Until Marriage]

If you're a Christian, you know God wants his kids living a pure lifestyle. I'm sure you've heard this more than a few times throughout your spiritual journey. Am I right? It pretty much gets inscribed into our foreheads as soon as we make the decision to follow Jesus: "God hates sex outside of marriage. So don't tick off God!"

If you're like most people, you've learned at least one thing along the way: *Purity is hard.* Believe me, I know! Try waiting until you're almost thirty-one; yeah, it pretty much sucks. It only gets worse if you're thirty-eight.

But you know what? The call for purity doesn't stop when you say, "I do." It continues into your marriage.

And sometimes, despite being naked — and active — with my wife on a regular basis, purity of mind and heart is still a battle. It will be a battle until I die [or until I become blind, deaf, and a quadriplegic]. I *think* all of those things would make the battle a little easier.

Some Old Testament couples were, in my opinion, hot. More than likely, Hollywood wouldn't have deemed these couples A-listers, but in the eyes of God, they certainly were. Here's the top four. [If you want to add your own HOT OT couple to this sidebar, feel free!]

FOUR: BOAZ AND RUTH

Our number four couple is none other than the second-most-talked-about couple out of the town of Bethlehem. I'm sure the Jewish tabloids had a ball telling the twelve tribes the story behind Ruth and Boaz. His strength and determination [his mom is said to have been a prostitute from Canaan[2]] combined with her loyalty and bravery [she hung around and helped her biddy-for-a-mother-in-law Naomi] make this lovers' tale one of the greatest of all biblical romances.

Why they are on the HOT list: Ruth's night of lying at Boaz's feet was hot. She had to be one of the most forward holy women of all biblical times.

The hottest verse that references them says: "I am Ruth thine handmaid: spread therefore thy skirt over thine handmaid; for thou art a near kinsman" (Ruth 3:9, KJV). I have no idea what all of that means, but it sounds hot. Some biblical scholars believe this verse is alluding to something sexual[3]; however, most do not. Either way, Ruth gets big kudos for being brave enough to get her man!

BONUS HOT: Boaz and Ruth are King David's great-grandparents. That's pretty cool, huh?

THREE: JACOB AND RACHEL

These young lovebirds met while watering sheep! Something must have been in the water that day because the town of Haran quickly became abuzz with speculation about when this new couple would marry. Before love could be consummated, Jacob would have quite a few hurdles to leap. But he wasn't about to let anything — not a conniving future father-in-law, not Rachel's very fertile sister who became Jacob's first wife, and not fourteen years of hard work — keep him from marrying the love of his life. *Mmm, now that's love.*

Why they are on the HOT list: Love that has overcome obstacles is just plain hot.

The hottest verse that references them says: "And he went in also unto Rachel, and he loved also Rachel more than Leah, and served with him yet seven other years" (Genesis 29:30, KJV).

BONUS HOT: Jacob and Rachel were the parents of Joseph — you know, the multicolored-coat guy!

TWO: ABRAHAM AND SARAH

The number two couple is none other than the great Abraham and Sarah. Despite being old, these two made sure the bed was still warm enough for some old lovin' from time to time. Christians, as well as Jews, should be thankful that A&S were still going at it in their old age. It was their passion for each other, along with the fact that nothing is impossible with God, that made it possible for the couple to be blessed with their son, Isaac.

Why they are on the HOT list: The combination of faith in God and a healthy sex life is always hot.

The hottest verse that references them says: "And he brought him forth abroad, and said, Look now toward heaven, and tell the stars, if thou be able to number them: and he said unto him, So shall thy seed be" (Genesis 15:5, KJV). Nothing is hotter than receiving a promise like that from God.

ONE: ADAM AND EVE

Coming in at the top spot are none other than the first man and woman, Adam and Eve! What wasn't hot about Adam and Eve? Running around naked, being the first two people to enjoy sexual intimacy, communing with God — it just doesn't get any better than that. And you know they probably "did it" all the time. It's not like they had to worry about the neighbors! And considering that they were formed out of the mouth of God, you know they/it/everything was hot. We'll be talking about them until the end of time!

Why they are on the HOT list: Guilt-free nudity. Lots of sex. *Very* hot.

The hottest verse that references them says: "And they were both naked, the man and his wife, and were not ashamed" (Genesis 2:25, KJV).

SIDEBAR BONUS: BRING BACK THE GOOD OLE DAYS!

Adam and Eve have inspired a brand-new generation of unashamed souls! That's right: Christian nudists are everywhere. Yes, you heard me correctly. Saved nudists do exist. These people love Jesus; they just love to serve him while in the nude. In an effort to bring back the "freedom" Adam and Eve experienced in the Garden of Eden, thousands of born-again Christians from all over the world are forming faith-based nudist colonies. *Yippee! You're excited, huh? [Yeah, probably not.]*

Okay, I have a question for you Jesus-loving nudists. When you evangelize, you at least wear socks and shoes, right? Gosh, not even heathens want your dirty feet walking on the living room carpet. [Just so you know, I'm not lying. Here's one such website: www.OurSunHome.com. And no, they don't show anything too R-rated. Hello? They're Christians!]

I've heard some Christians make purity sound so simple. With so many of us, it's all about the package. Too often, we're consumed with finding the easiest way from point A to point B. When it comes to things of a sexual nature, the church sometimes is quick to package purity like it's a box you can buy or simple directions you can follow. I admit that I've wanted this before. I've looked spiritual people in the eye and said, "Just give me a list of rules and I'll follow them!" And Christian culture is not short on rules; we have lots of them. Of course, the rules work for a season but don't prove effective in the end. I don't know about you, but I always ended up breaking the rules.

But despite purity not being easy, most Christians who are engaged in their faith desire it, and they should. God throughout the Old Testament and Jesus in the New Testament spoke candidly about the call for humanity to strive toward purity. Pursuing a healthy and holy sexual lifestyle is much bigger and deeper and all consuming than most imagine. The following is a list of what I believe the Bible says to be true about striving toward a lifestyle of purity.

It's a sacrifice. Sex has been happening outside of God's parameters almost since the beginning of time. Before you can truly feel the weight of this calling to chaste behavior, you have to know that your decision to wait—and then remain faithful within your marriage—is indeed a lifelong sacrifice. You must decide whether or not surrendering to God's desire is important to you. Sure, the fear of pregnancy or getting a sexually transmitted disease or being labeled a *non*virgin are great reasons to wait, but you're fooling yourself if you think they will keep you from having sex outside of marriage. *They won't.* A person's desire to live a chaste lifestyle—inside and outside of marriage—must come from the core of who he or she is. If this decision is not coming from your spiritual center—in other words, solely embracing, surrendering, and engaging the things of Jesus—you're probably not realizing the sacrifice it takes to make this call a lifestyle and not simply something you do until you get married. Because I hate to break it to you, but this sacrifice doesn't stop or even get easier within marriage.

Surrendering is a continuous struggle. Some of you have signed a petition saying you will wait to have sex until marriage. Others of you have committed a bunch a sexual screwups and with real emotion and sincere conviction have taken your deepest confessions to a church and then promised you wouldn't ever do whatever you've done again. You'd probably do yourself a good favor by resisting emotionally driven promises unless you're able to view the "come to Jesus" event as simply a jumping-off point. Because this sacrifice — the forfeiting of one thing for another thing considered to be of greater value — is continuous; it requires our ongoing participation, our ongoing surrender.

True love serves, makes mistakes, forgives, and tries again. I think it's flawed thinking to say that true love waits. This thinking puts too much emphasis on the act of sex. What happens if a couple makes a mistake? Does that instantly mean love didn't exist? Does that mean their love wasn't true? *I don't think so.* Always remember what 1 Corinthians 13:4-8 says:

> Love is patient and kind. Love is not jealous or boastful or proud or rude. Love does not demand its own way. Love is not irritable, and it keeps no record of when it has been wronged. It is never glad about injustice but rejoices whenever the truth wins out. Love never gives up, never loses faith, is always hopeful, and endures through every circumstance. Love will last forever. (NLT)

If these attributes are true after marriage, then they're true before marriage, too. True love cannot be defined by an event; it must be defined by the journey both lead.

It requires a companion. Don't walk this journey alone. Don't even assume you can walk this journey alone. You can't. Whether you're male, female, young, old, married, or single, this journey requires companions; it requires people you can trust who will guide you toward the right path, support you when you're struggling, and be hope-filled when you fall. *Please!* Don't walk alone.

Sacrifice, surrender, true love, and journeying with a companion are all really DIFFICULT. Don't fool yourself. A healthy and holy lifestyle is difficult even when you're playing with all the pieces. You must be free enough to bask in grace. Remember, perfection is *not* the goal, nor is it possible. So when you do screw up, don't sign another petition or make another empty promise, but confess, be hopeful, and know that there is no condemnation

Jesus Said:

"You know the next commandment pretty well, too: 'Don't go to bed with another's spouse.' But don't think you've preserved your virtue simply by staying out of bed. Your *heart* can be corrupted by lust even quicker than your *body*. Those leering looks you think nobody notices — they also corrupt.

"Let's not pretend this is easier than it really is. If you want to live a morally pure life, here's what you have to do: You have to blind your right eye the moment you catch it in a lustful leer. You have to choose to live one-eyed or else be dumped on a moral trash pile. And you have to chop off your right hand the moment you notice it raised threateningly. Better a bloody stump than your entire being discarded for good in the dump."

(Matthew 5:27-30)

for those who are in Christ. Purity is *impossible* without Jesus.

A friend teaches me something.

Tom has been my friend for a while now. His wise words have encouraged me often during the last seven years of my spiritual journey. As soon as I met him — he was leading worship music at a fundraiser — I knew he would be a man who could have a great deal of spiritual influence in my life. As a former Young Life leader, this fiftysomething had seen and experienced a lot. It seemed to me that his experiences had only brought him closer to the truth.

Sex was a topic that Tom and I talked about often. He was a sounding board for all of my frustrations, screwups, and confessions. I didn't feel the need to hold back when talking to him; Tom heard it all. After I blurted out my life stories, Tom would usually smirk and then offer some of the wisest words I'd ever heard. It wasn't as though his thoughts broke new ground. But for me, they didn't have to. He simply and graciously pointed me back to the truth.

One of those conversations has proved most important for my life. After having ended another relationship, one of those that came to an end because I had "gone too far" and felt too much guilt to continue, I looked at Tom and said, "I'm so d%#@ sick of going through the same ridiculous routine, only

Spontaneous Game Time

Can you connect the Old Testament celebrity with his or her sexual fame?
[Answers are below.]

My OT Celebrity Name	My Fame
1. David	A. My story is often used as a case *against* masturbation.
2. Rahab	B. One of my three sons walked in on me drunk and naked. I cursed him.
3. Solomon	C. My spouse and I were the first couple to get it on. Yes, it was *good*.
4. Adam	D. I slept at the foot of my crush's bed and scored a mate.
5. Lot	E. I'm the prostitute who saved the spies.
6. Noah	F. You think I know the *secret* to great sex because I had three hundred wives.
7. Joseph	G. I'm the good-hearted king who slept with another man's wife.
8. Onan	H. I helped govern the city God destroyed for its sexual promiscuity.
9. Ruth	I. I resisted my employer's wife's sexual advances. But I still got put in jail.

ANSWERS: (1) G, (2) E, (3) F, (4) C, (5) H, (6) B, (7) I, (8) A, (9) D

to end up making another mistake." Tom didn't wince at my story; he simply watched me talk without *ever* interrupting. Only when I had finished telling my story did Tom speak; his words were abrupt and unbridled but always heartfelt.

"Matthew, should I call your *now* ex-girlfriend and get her side of the story?" he asked with a chuckle. "Because I'm sure it's a little different from yours."

We both laughed but he more than me.

"I've told you this before, Matthew," said Tom. "Every time we get together, I hear a young man who wants to live life passionately and faithfully. I like that about you. However, when it comes to sex, my friend, you're a mixed-up mess. And the truth is, I'm not sure you truly believe the pure life, or perhaps I should say God's way of doing things, is truly the best life to be lived. You're not convinced he knows best. You've certainly seen evidence in your story that it is; we all see that from time to time. However, you live your life like you still believe you know the answers. All you're doing is walking in and out of relationships, leaving a long line of hurt and guilty feelings in your path. In order for a Jesus-follower to truly engage the holy lifestyle, he must first believe that following God's path is best. Can you sit here and tell me you truly believe that the sex life God outlines in Scripture is best?"

I stared at Tom, not really knowing what to say. My mind chased a million thoughts, but I kept coming back to just one: Tom was right; at that time, I didn't truly believe God's way was best. I was basically living a parody of the Christian life.

"How do you believe something that rarely seems to work?" I asked.

"Faith," said Tom. "It takes faith. Scripture teaches that people with true faith follow God and his Word blindly, not because they can *see* it's the best but simply because God *said* it was best. Before you can live out purity, you must first believe it's the best life. Of course, believing won't guarantee you'll always make the right decision, but at least you'll have the right foundation."

Tom looked at me and smiled. I just stared at him with a knowing grin.

"I wish it were simple, Matthew," he said. "But you know the old saying: 'The right way is almost always difficult.'"

That day's conversation was the beginning of a changed perspective for me regarding sex. I walked away knowing that in order for me to truly pursue a holy and healthy lifestyle, I first had to believe that holy and healthy was the best way to live. Instead of going into relationships wondering how long I could go without screwing up, I needed to ask God for the faith to believe that his foundation of purity was indeed the best way to live.

Do you believe God's way is best? Yes, I know this sounds like I'm getting ready to have an old-fashioned altar call. I promise you, I'm not.

However, I do believe it's important for all of us to ask ourselves whether we believe God's design for our sex life is truly the best sex life we could have. Like Tom told me, believing doesn't make the road easier or free of mistakes, but it does ensure we have a foundation to stand on, run back to, and build on. A lot of us don't have any foundation because deep down, we doubt that God truly knows what he's talking about. We don't believe his way is best. Or we don't believe in it enough to make sacrifices.

You probably know how babies are made. Well, you know the "main ingredients" anyway. But you may need to know a little more when the time comes for you and your spouse to create one. So as a brief refresher, here are six easy steps to remember. [Of course, this assumes you have met the man or woman of your dreams, gotten married, and are having wild, passionate, unprotected sex — after all, why would you use birth control if you were trying to make a baby?]

1 Each month a woman ovulates, which essentially means her body releases a tiny egg. You can only see a female's egg with a microscope. It's not like a chicken; they don't come in dozens.

2 The egg travels to the fallopian tube, waiting for a single sperm to penetrate it. It is important to note that the egg can only be fertilized for about twenty-four hours after ovulation. Typically, this all takes place about two weeks after a woman's menstrual period.

3 When the sperm penetrates the egg and fertilizes it [kind of like Miracle-Gro], the baby's genetic makeup is complete, including its sex. [NOTE: Men determine the sex of the baby. Women can only provide X chromosomes, so if the sperm is an X, the baby will be a girl, but if the sperm is a Y, the baby will be a boy.]

4 Within twenty-four hours after fertilization, the egg begins dividing like crazy into numerous cells while it's still in the fallopian tube. After about three days, the fertilized egg, which is now called a zygote, passes out of the fallopian tube and into the uterus.

5 The zygote becomes a solid ball of cells and then a hollow ball of cells before implanting itself in the uterus.

6 Presto! A baby has been made, and he or she will develop into a little "you" over the next nine months. Then the delivery process will take place, but that is a chapter for another book.

Doesn't all of this baby talk get you excited? Yeah, I thought so. Say this: Diapers are fun. Now repeat it three times and see if it still sounds fun.

Welcome to the Real World

[the BIG issues and questions Christians have regarding sex]

> Mortal lovers must not try to remain at the first step; for lasting passion is the dream of a harlot and from it we wake in despair.
>
> — C. S. Lewis

As I began to dissect the topic of sex, it felt somewhat similar to what my science teacher might have experienced when he decided to dissect a dog's testicle in my tenth-grade biology class. You're probably thinking, *This is random.* Yes, it is. But dissecting sex and dissecting a dog's testicle do relate to some degree. First off, you're completely shocked by the wealth of innuendos available on the topic. You'd be pretty surprised at how often and to what extent a group of tenth graders can relate everyday life to a dog's testicle. But the same is true for sex; the innuendos are endless. Of course, I've tried to be good while writing this book, but sometimes you just can't help letting one fly now and again.

When my teacher began to cut open the doggie's ball, the girls screeched and the boys marveled. None of us had any clue as to what we'd find hidden inside. All I know is that my teacher was WAY fascinated by this testicle. Like only an overexcited science teacher can, he explained each characteristic with such detail and delight that you'd have thought we were discovering a new solar system inside the dog's little guy.

But alas, it was just the inside of a canine's gonad.

Dissecting sex as it relates to Christians is, in my assessment, a bit more exciting than cutting into an object that once dangled between a dog's hind legs, but that's just because of the sexual complexities involved. The sexual real world of Christians has many layers to it, just like the testicle, and this section will attempt to cut through a few of them and will hopefully give you a little something to grab on to. [Now, that was an innuendo.]

Christians, Sex, and Sexual Activity

Okay, so I'm just going to blurt it out: A lot of unmarried Christians are engaging in sexual activity. [*YIKES!*] Yes, it's true; they are.

Let me guess; you're now wishing this section was about the dog's testicle, right?

I know; you weren't expecting such devastating news right at the beginning of section 3, huh? Some of you might be shocked. But most of you aren't surprised at all.

But before I get into the juicy details of this chapter, first things first. . . .

YES, YES, and YES.

No, I don't have literary Tourette's syndrome. If I did, I would hope my random writings would be something much more vivid, creative, and exclamatory than "yes." So why did I write three yesses in a row? They are meant to answer the three questions running through some of your minds right now.

Yes, the Christians who are having sex are *real* Christians, not merely "pseudo-Christians." They aren't what some evangelicals like to call "Oprah" Christians.

Yes, these Christians are actually engaged in their faith when they slip up and then in and out, as the case usually is.

And yes, the "activity" I speak of includes not only sexual intercourse but also oral sex and mutual masturbation. I'm not sure there's anything more romantic sounding than the term mutual masturbation. [Insert sarcasm. 😵]

If you've read the statistics—at least the few available involving Christian young adults' penises and vaginas—you probably know what they say about the sexual lifestyle of Christians. Most of the studies I've found reveal that although Christians wait longer to engage in sexual activity and engage with fewer partners than non-Christians, exploration of "sexual healing" prior to marriage is indeed happening. One study that included young adults in its findings came out in 2003. The Barna Group, a Christian research company, found that 42 percent of Christians [people of faith calling themselves evangelical or born-again] believed that sex outside of marriage was acceptable.[1] [*BUT* this study is slightly tainted since it included subjects from a very wide range of ages. Certainly not a bad study, but not truly helpful for this book because it reveals only what Christians believe and not how they act.*]

Unfortunately, most of the available studies center on Christian teenagers and sex. There seems to be a lot of Christians who have this "let's get 'em out of high school untouched and they'll be fine" theory. A lot of information regarding the sexual habits of twentysomething and thirty-something single/dating Christians is available, but often it's not in the form of scientific statistics.

Now it's time for an introduction.

Dr. Brandon Hill [this guy is official ☺] is the dean of students at Point Loma Nazarene University. I learned of Dr. Hill through his editorial work at the website http://chris-tianteens.about.com. [He creates content and answers teenagers' questions at this site.] When I contacted him for an interview, I was pleasantly surprised to learn that Dr. Hill had recently finished some extensive research on the sexual habits

---

* *It might be important to note that this study also found that what Barna defined as morality was on the decline among Christians. Sadly, I'm not sure we needed a survey to tell us this information.*

of Christian guys. His sample included two hundred students from one Christian university. Here is a list of some of his theories and the conclusions he determined from his study:

⇨ "It appears that Christian students think that everything but intercourse is all right."

⇨ "Three percent admitted to being homosexual or bisexual. Slightly higher numbers reported actual homosexual activity [mutual masturbation, oral sex, anal sex]."

⇨ "The corporate desire for virginity is on the decline."

⇨ "There was a very high frequency of both masturbation and pornography."

⇨ "The research indicated a fairly quick progression from lesser [physical] activities [kissing and making out] to the more intimate sexual activities [ones including nudity or stimulated orgasm]."

But statistics, no matter how accurate, often fail to tell the story behind the behavior. So in order to get a better idea of what Christian young adults' sex lives are like, I went to the source. As I stated earlier in the book, I surveyed people who identified themselves as followers of Jesus and asked them questions about their sexual activity. Though these survey results are not scientific, they do reveal a rather descriptive narrative about the struggles Christians experience in the area of sexuality before they make their marriage vows. The following is a list of answers I received when I asked this question: "Have you been sexually active? If so, to what extent?"

- ⊃ "I've never had actual intercourse but have given and received oral sex." — *Traci, 25*
- ⊃ "I haven't done much, a little foreplay with my boyfriend, but not intercourse." — *Shawna, 27*
- ⊃ "My first sexual experience was with a girl; I've made out before with guys, but it never got that far." — *Stephanie, 30*
- ⊃ "I dated a girl who was a young Christian, not good. We never connected for intercourse or oral, but did stimulate each other until climax." — *Devon, 25*
- ⊃ "Yep, I've had sex — *lots of it.*" — *Tori, 22*
- ⊃ "I've given and received oral sex." — *Trent, 18*
- ⊃ "Nope." — *Terrance, 22*
- ⊃ "I've done nothing except make out with three girls." — *Brandon, 27*
- ⊃ "Umm, well, I've felt and licked a lot of places, but I'm still a virgin." — *Richard, 21*
- ⊃ "I'm sexually active with my boyfriend to the extent that we engage in mutual masturbation and oral sex." — *Samantha, 21*
- ⊃ "I've had one sexual partner. It didn't last long. The relationship was built on sex and sexual pleasure, but we were too f&^%$@ up and not committed to making it last." — *Henry, 28*

What You Didn't Learn from Your Parents About Sex Presents:
Answers to Your Most Intriguing Sex Questions!

QUESTION: "Is it possible to tell a person's virginity status just by looking at them?"
— James, 24, Christian rock star

ANSWER: Good question, James. We love this question! You might be surprised to learn how many people write us about this very topic. Jessica Simpson has inquired about it at least five times. Unfortunately, I wish the answer were as easy as she is. As you might know, people have been arguing about this topic for many years now. During medieval times, some claimed a woman's virginity could be determined by the direction her breasts pointed. Up, she was. Down, she wasn't. But James, we have an answer for you. Depending on your personal worldview, here are three potential answers

Wow. Now you've got a small taste as to why the topic of sex is so complex and multi-layered. For me, one thing was obviously clear when reading through the surveys. Christians have a lot of questions, frustrations, and excitement about sex. And that's why we're getting ready to do a little digging into some of the issues surrounding sexuality and being Christian.

Masturbation

[A section for 95 percent of men, 70 percent of women, and a bunch of liars]

It probably doesn't come as a huge surprise that one of the biggest issues in the minds [and hands] of Christians is masturbation.

People masturbate. Christians included. *Are you surprised?* Of course you're not surprised. Sure, there are a few of you who have never done such an act. But certainly most have. If you're one of those who have never mastur-bated, you might not be familiar with the term's definition. I find this highly unlikely, but you never know when someone is a Christian. Being sheltered is often a major part of the "saved" territory. So don't feel strange if you're not aware.

First, this is how dictionary.com defines masturbation: "Excitation of one's own or another's genital organs, usually

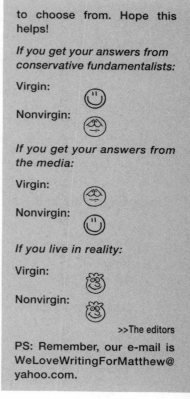

to choose from. Hope this helps!

If you get your answers from conservative fundamentalists:

Virgin:

Nonvirgin:

If you get your answers from the media:

Virgin:

Nonvirgin:

If you live in reality:

Virgin:

Nonvirgin:

>>The editors

PS: Remember, our e-mail is WeLoveWritingForMatthew@yahoo.com.

to orgasm, by manual contact or means other than sexual intercourse." [But this section won't focus on the "you touching another" portion of masturbation. Just the "one's own" part.]

This topic gets chatted about *a lot* in the world of Christian culture. Small groups analyze it. Accountability partners pray about it. Books discuss it. Elder boards form opinions about it. Conference speakers touch on it. [Hee hee.] Friends confide in each other about it. And counselors shed light on it.

But let's face it: When we're alone, most of us do it [or have done it].

Let's start things off with a brief history of masturbation.

Masturbation is indeed a popular pastime, and most historians believe that it's been popular since the beginning.

But wait; before you get feisty and write me a hateful letter, I want to be sure you know this: I am in no way suggesting that Adam masturbated. *He may have.* But I have NO way of knowing. And you don't either, really. But despite not knowing whether the first man and woman took matters into their own hands, some people believe history does imply that the M-word has been an issue from the beginning. It might be helpful to discuss what history we do think we know, or at least what somebody thinks he knows:

➤ **From the beginning?** Apparently the Central African Bonobo chimpanzees masturbate. I didn't know this, but they share 85 to 90 percent of our human DNA.[2] [*Wow. That 10 to 15 percent must really make a difference.*] According to evolutionists, this supposedly provides some confirmation that masturbation has been practiced since the beginning of time.[3] Perhaps now I understand why scientists call it the BIG BANG theory, but I wouldn't quote me on that.

➤ **Those crazy BC Egyptians** celebrated masturbation as the process by which their sun god, Atum, created the Egyptian equivalents to Adam and Eve. I had never heard this before, but apparently their names were Shu and Tefnut. There's even a quote: "With [his hand], Atun masturbated and brought forth the first pair of souls." [Oh yeah, and there's a scary etching, too —*I didn't need to see that.*][4]

➤ **You're not ready for this one!** Ladies, you might want to close your eyes as you read this. The Sumerians, who invented the first written Western language, suggest a masturbation habit was a proud quality of their Mesopotamian god Enki. [Would you follow any god named Enki? I don't know about you, but to me it sounds like sushi. "I would like to order the ENKI, please!"] Legend has it, and this is where it gets gross, that this great god's ejaculation filled the Tigris River.[5] *Yeah. Sick!*

➤ **Fast-forward a few thousand years.** In the 1700s and 1800s, masturbation began being associated with mental and physical deficiencies. *This might explain Walt Whitman.* It's estimated that up to 60 percent of mental and physical illnesses were blamed on masturbation.[6]

➤ **Yeah, so the fear of masturbation** became so great that the "cereal guru" John Harvey Kellogg proclaimed that sex, for any reason other than reproduction, was "sexual excess."[7] Okay, so let me get this straight: People actually took sex advice from the guy who invented Corn Flakes and Frosted Mini-Wheats? *Seems like a grrrrRREEEEEAAT plan to me.*

Unfortunately, a lot [certainly not all] of the eighteenth- and nineteenth-century thinking perpetuated from Christians or "the religious." I know; you, like me, are completely shocked that Christians would do such a thing! But sadly, it's true. Many God-followers have long tried to impose their staunch feelings about this controversial topic onto the lives of humanity. However, the medical community didn't help matters much either. In the early twentieth century, some doctors invented devices—yes, devices—to help men and women refrain from masturbating. These devices had names like The Cage, Dr. Moodie's Aparatus for Boys, Sexual Armor, and The Spike-Lined Device.[8]

And I thought cold showers were bad.

Thankfully, religious and medical communities have learned a thing or two from our old mistakes and theories. But even some of today's Christians make a huge fuss about masturbation. You don't believe me? Just do a Google search on the topic. It's actually uncanny how much time Christians invest in talking about, debating, worrying about, and "curing" masturbation. I guess I have no room to talk; I've spent the better part of a month researching it. But at least you won't have to! By the amount of information, questions, and fears [from both men and women] displayed online, you might think the only thing some Christians do is masturbate, feel horribly guilty about it, start a forum online about their feelings, get some advice from other strugglers, and then masturbate again. [If you think I'm exaggerating, check out Crosswalk.com's "men only" forum.][9]

It really has been quite educational for me to read about people's thoughts regarding this ancient habit. Of course, I knew people had questions and worries; I've certainly had a few of my own along the way.

But I believe there's a silver lining that comes with all of this talking; it implies that people are beginning to feel more comfortable discussing the topic. And in my opinion, that's a very good thing. However, I think the good greatly depends on where their information is coming from. Because today, the Christian views about "self-relieving sexual tension" are all across the board.

Almost all the contemporary views differ greatly from those our Founding Fathers might have believed. Today's views of masturbation range from adamant opposition [but thankfully without the use of "devices"] to calling it "a gift that a loving and gracious God has given."[10] And because of the Internet, everybody's views and perspectives get equal play [or at least are heard]—from professional counselors and journalists to bloggers and pastors. Consider these current Christian ideas about masturbation. Then you and I will talk again several paragraphs later!

→ **The "you're digging a big ole ditch" theory.** "Basically, you should not masturbate or look or think about your male body because of how highly reinforcing masturbation is." That's what Jayson Graves, Christian psychotherapist (www.healingforthesoul.org), thinks about the topic. Mr. Graves, who works every day with those suffering from sexual addiction, believes that every time men masturbate, they are conditioning—or hard-wiring—their brains for addiction. He wrote this statement in an article called "Sex and the Brain": "Imagine if you were to dig a ditch between the street and sidewalk from your driveway down to the store on the corner. Every day you walk in that ditch to buy the morning paper and over time that ditch gets deeper and wider to the point where even if you wanted to walk on the street or sidewalk, because of the erosion, there would be a tendency to fall back into the ditch. THIS IS THE ADDICTION."

→ **Blogging Bonnie's theory [this one even comes with a new term!].** Sometimes those who post comments and opinions about masturbation online come up with *new* terms or ideas to describe the act. Over the years, I've heard Christians use nonslang terms like "solo sex" and "self-sex." One guy, a well-loved Christian radio personality, believed masturbation was a form of homosexuality [because you're "having sex with the same sex"—you]. But Bonnie, a blogging mother of three from New York with a website at http://takeanumberplease.blogspot.com, calls masturbation something I had never heard before: autoerotism. [*Sounds like a really strange act involving a car.*] Her view is this: "Can it truthfully be said that autoerotism brings one closer to God, or, at the very least, does not separate one from God, if it indeed represents a use of sex for which it was not designed?" In her post about autoerotism, Bonnie also includes a little angst toward Dr. James Dobson's point of view. "I have read James Dobson's thoughts on the subject," writes Bonnie. "[I] find them surprising and disappointing. It is odd that someone so hard-line on other issues of sexual morality can simply brush this one aside."

→ **Doc's theory.** Speaking of Dr. Dobson, his view at www .family.org is outlined in the form of a response to a parent's concern that her thirteen-year-old is doing the "deed." After a long pontification about the "four concerning circumstances" surrounding stimulating oneself—which include overwhelming guilt, extreme obsessive masturbatory behavior, addiction to pornographic material, and the effects it can have on a healthy sexual lifestyle within marriage—Dr. Dobson gets personal. Well, at least for him, this is personal: "My mother and father discussed this subject with me. We were riding in the car, and my dad said, 'Jim, when I was a boy, I worried so much about masturbation. It really became a scary thing for me because I thought God was condemning me for what I couldn't help. So I'm telling you now that I hope you don't feel the need to engage in this act when you reach the teen years, but if you do, you shouldn't be too concerned about it. I don't believe it has much to do with your relationship with God.' What a kind thing my father did for me that night in the car." What a kind thing Dr. Dobson would do for a lot of kids and adults if he told that story every day on his radio program. Well, maybe not every day, but at least once a month.

→ **The "rise and shine and give God the glory" theory.** While I was an editor at *CCM Magazine*, *Youth Worker Journal*, a then-sister magazine to *CCM*, ran a controversial op-ed piece about masturbation. It caused quite a stir among youth ministries across the country. Some praised the piece's frank, honest, and open-minded view. Others responded, calling it "rubbish." Dr. Dale Kaufman, a youth ministry veteran and author of "Is Masturbation a Sin?" wrote this in the feature: "Is it possible to masturbate without straying into sinful thoughts? The answer is yes; for God, in designing the human body, has given it the ability to respond to physical stimuli without the necessity of embracing sinful thought. And it's all right to enjoy the pleasurable feelings that accompany the activity." But he didn't stop there. He went on to say this: "And if the thought life is kept under control, the act becomes an experience of blessing from the Lord, rather than a shameful one. The sin [comes] in abusing a gift that a loving and gracious God has given." And he might have gotten away with his controversial point of view had he not gone here: "After [Johnny (a kid Dr. Kauffman referenced throughout the feature)] heard about the boundaries [of masturbation] written in Scriptures and realized that God wasn't going to condemn him for what he had done, Johnny began to come to a new understanding of how God wanted him to use the act of masturbation to bring glory to [him]. Johnny was amazed that he could thank God for the pleasure he was experiencing, and how such a focus of keeping his eyes on Jesus and keeping his thought life under control—while at the same time enjoying the sensations and giving God the praise—would be a tremendous help to him and would alleviate the false guilt he had been experiencing."[11] *Yeah, so the whole "praising God" part didn't go over too well. But it did get people thinking.*

Okay, so maybe you're wondering why I'm sharing four *very* distinct views. I did this because I think it's important for you to know that faith-based views do exist today. And there are certainly more opinions—hundreds more—but I believe most other Christian opinions could simply become subpoints under these four that I mention.

But from my research—what I have read online, the surveys I received from individuals, and my conversations with friends and counselors—one thing becomes quite clear about masturbation and how it relates to Christians: Twentysomethings and thirtysomethings struggle with knowing what they should believe to be true.

Here's what we know:

> Most do it.
> Some feel guilty about it.
> Some don't.
> Such a strange predicament this issue
> puts so many people in.

Personally . . .

Some of this section might make a few of you uncomfortable. [If you're my mother, look away. *In fact, just skip to the last section, Mom.*]

Okay, it's time to share a personal story.

I think I was fifteen when I, umm, you know, partook of the *topic* I'm discussing right now. [I don't know why, but it's hard to write the word when I'm telling a story about myself.] Anyway, when it happened, I thought I had broken something. In fact, I worried for more than a week about what I had done and whether or not it would have long-term effects on my ability to have children, make love to my future wife, or even pee. I'm sure this doesn't happen to most people. However, even if you can't exactly relate, most would agree that the first time a kid achieves an orgasm it can be an experience that is exhilarating, frightening, and embarrassing.

Of course, after the guilt, fear, and embarrassment passes, it's normal to be curious about whether or not what happened the first time would/could/should happen again. So our hormone-driven curiosity drives us to explore again [and usually again and again].

Masturbation can become quite the habit. Friends have

How to Resist Temptation?!?

[three ideas that might help you fight the good fight — I said *might*]

THREE: RUN! You can't simply run. Nor should you walk fast. If you want to seriously outfox temptation, you must RUN! It must be the kind of running that requires all caps and an exclamation point. Anything less and you're sinning.

TWO: Emergency excuse. Everyone needs an emergency excuse. An escape method is a must just in case you're surprised by temptation. Perhaps it could be, "Darn, I have to go home and feed my puppy." Or maybe, "Oh my gosh, I must leave now; I have a roast in the oven!" If you find yourself in the midst of fighting temptation and you can't remember your emergency excuse, then RUN! like Jackie Joyner-Kersee.

ONE: Fake a seizure. Please note: This method should be used only in extreme emergencies. Fall

told me that at times in their life, they would do it two or three times a day. *Who has that kind of time?* However, my friends' stories were always much more about lust or porn or guilt than they were about masturbation.

In high school, it wasn't that way for me. Lust was not a force that I dealt with much. Sure, I thought about girls and wondered what a female body might feel like to touch. And I certainly wouldn't have looked away if a girl in a bikini walked by me. I wasn't a pure little angel. But my thoughts about women didn't control me; they weren't playing over and over in my mind like a bad R-rated movie. I certainly wasn't addicted to the act of *partaking*. I didn't *partake* because of dirty thoughts or a lust-filled heart; in high school, I did it because it felt good. Period.

So I raise the question: Is it a sin to masturbate? *In some instances I believe it is.* Is it always a sin? *I don't think so.* Is it possible to do it without lusting and without pornography? *Yes.* However, you might feel otherwise.

down. Begin shaking uncontrollably. If possible, saliva should be protruding from between your lips. But don't overdo it. Since seizures can appear scary to others around you, all sinning or temptation to sin should instantly dissipate.

Some of you are really mad at me right now because you've always felt like your masturbation habits are sinful. So you believe that by saying it's not always sinful, I'm giving you permission to continue in your sin. Well, I think it's important to understand that if you believe it's a sin for you, then you need to follow what your conscience is telling you. Masturbation is an issue between you and your conscience. I don't want you to use my opinion as a way to excuse your actions.

Besides, I'm not ready to shout from the mountaintops, "I GUARANTEE THAT MASTURBATION IS NOT A SIN!" Because truthfully, I don't know. *Nobody knows.* God never mentioned it. However, if it had been an abomination to him, I truly believe he would have mentioned it; he would have put it in Scripture somewhere. He certainly mentioned a lot of other things.

But I will say this: I think a lot of Christians spend way too much time debating, concentrating on, and judging masturbation. Sure, I think it's a topic that should be discussed in a proper forum. But I don't believe we need to be consumed with it. And some of us are.

I've experienced times in my life when it consumed me. There have been times when I felt so much guilt over masturbation that I was hardly able to concentrate on work, relationships, and service. I've given it up for Lent—and made it twenty-nine days. I've had accountability for it numerous times, and usually that would become the only thing we'd discuss. Do you know how many times I've had a good friend of mine look at me and ask, "So, Matthew, did you do it this week?"

I find this a little ridiculous.

Does the church really need to be the masturbation police? If someone feels he or she is addicted, then yes, I want that person to feel comfortable enough to express his or her problem with someone at the church. But do we really need to make husbands, wives, college students, and teenagers consumed with thoughts over this issue?

What does consuming people with something God doesn't talk about *truly* accomplish?

Do I want to be pure? YES. Do I want to have a mind that is holy? ABSOLUTELY. Do I want to have to tell three or four of my close guy friends every time I masturbate? Not really.

Wouldn't it be more Christian if we had accountability partners who asked us about our service to the poor? Jesus mentioned the poor hundreds of times. He never mentioned masturbation.

However, despite having a strong opinion about how the church often deals with this issue, I'm certainly not going to tell you how you should live your life. I don't know your struggles. And we're all responsible for our own actions. I'm simply going to break this issue down for you in facts. Once you know the facts, it's your responsibility to seek Jesus on the issue to ask him how you should live. Whatever you hear him saying to your heart I believe you should obey, regardless of anyone else's opinion. Just make sure your conviction is built on what Jesus is telling you and is not driven by lies or guilt. And most important, pursue purity with passion.

Here are the facts:

- Ninety-five percent of men have masturbated; 70 percent of women have masturbated.
- Masturbation is not mentioned in Scripture—not by Abraham, not by Paul, and not by Jesus.

- ⟡ The *act* of masturbation has no long-term mental, emotional, or spiritual effects on a person. Those who suggest otherwise are probably not talking about the effects of masturbation as much as they are talking about outside factors that often go along with a masturbation habit [i.e., pornography and sex addiction].
- ⟡ The Bible is clear that lust [of any kind] is wrong.
- ⟡ Most medical professionals believe masturbation to be a normal and healthy part of adolescence.
- ⟡ Some Christian spiritual leaders believe that the *guilt* Christians feel because of masturbation is much more damaging than masturbation could ever be.
- ⟡ An individual *can* be addicted to masturbation. But again, most sexual addictions that involve masturbation are usually perpetuated by an outside factor such as lust, pornography, sexual history, or other circumstances.
- ⟡ Most important, remember you can't out-*sin* the grace of Jesus. It's impossible.

Sex Help!

In case you need something to think about *instead* of masturbation, why not think about butterflies? Butterflies are cool.

Pornography

[you've heard it's addictive; let's discuss why]

Okay, so in high school lust wasn't an issue for me, but in college, that changed.

The feeling of lust wasn't something I experienced until my second year of college. My first taste of how good lust can feel was through pornography. I had long known about porn; I had been inside our town's video store. I was the kid who would judge those sneaking back into the "special room." On one occasion I saw an older man I knew from church emerge from that room; I never told a soul. I just avoided him; he was a *sinner*.

Up until my second year at college, I'd never been tempted to buy pornography. I had been

Four FOOLPROOF Ways to Stop the MADNESS!

So you want to stop masturbating? *Completely?* Are you sure? Well, I have some great suggestions for you!

1. Cut off your hands. I know this seems drastic, but don't get upset with me; Jesus suggested it first.

2. Live life in handcuffs. Again, this might be awkward at first, but you'd get used to it. And it's A LOT less costly than what Jesus had in mind — amputation is *expensive*. And also, once you're married — well, you know.

3. Attach an electric pet collar to your genitalia and the "reactor" to your wrists. Whenever you're tempted to go for the action, you will instead experience sensations of another kind. Eventually, through trial and error, you'll learn how *close* you can get without being zapped; at least, dogs eventually learn. One problem though: Peeing can be rather unsafe with this option.

4. Get spayed or neutered. Anything Bob Barker advertises has to be good. And in a couple of years, with medical technology moving so quickly, the procedure will probably be reversible. I think you should *totally* do it. Hey, what is faith for?

FINE PRINT: This book is not responsible for any persons who fail to see the humor in this sidebar and actually attempt the actions listed above. But the book would like to express this sentiment: If you fry your genitals, you're an idiot. And we mean that with complete Christian love.

around it only once and, at the time, resisted the temptation to look.

Only when it became available in limited fashion on the Internet did I see it. I looked for just a couple of minutes that first time. But the few minutes I spent looking and reading were more than enough to make me feel guilty and dirty, like I had suddenly, right in the middle of my college's library, turned into a child molester, a rapist, or a dirty old man.

Of course, it's funny how quickly you forget those horrible feelings. Lust has a way of making you fail to remember them. The only things you end up remembering are the images you saw and the words you read, which make you want to go back for more.

Once the idea of pornography gets inside your mind, the curiosity for more is almost numbing. Sure, you garner enough strength to resist the urge a time or two, but the temptation just gets stronger. Over the years, I have shared my pornography experiences with both Christians and non-Christians. And through these conversations, I have come to believe that the urge to delve into the world of porn is often more overwhelming and alluring for Christians. Because we're often raised in a sheltered environment, when we come across something tempting and seemingly wonderful, it's like we've uncovered a new world that we feel must be explored. Consequently, because the lure is at times irresistible, we're quick to make like Lewis and Clark and blaze a trail through unchartered territory. Heck, sometimes we draw ourselves a map.

The difference between pornography and erotica is lighting.
—Gloria Leonard

The Reasons Behind Porn
[why it's so alluring]

I'm pretty darn sure you already know a hundred reasons why you shouldn't invest in pornography; I know the same ones. We could probably recite them together if given the chance.

But I have a question.

If it's true that we've memorized the reasons, why then do so many Christians—both men and women—find such retreat and comfort in pornography [and, often, in masturbation by itself]? I mean, most of us know what God says about holiness; we've read the Bible. The concepts of holiness have been hammered down our throats since we were kids.

But why then is porn so tempting?

Do I have to quote a bunch of Scripture verses to prove to you that pornography is wrong? I doubt it. The dreams God has for our sex lives are much sweeter than anything offered at an adults-only website. You've heard that before, right? I'm sure someone has shared with you God's dream for your sex life.

Why do you think we fail to believe it's true? Is God's design for sexuality really better than what you or I could experience outside of his plan wandering through the "wilderness"? It's supposed to be. But sometimes it certainly doesn't feel this way. Sometimes [maybe most of the time] it's much simpler taking our own road.

So we go looking elsewhere to satisfy the emptiness we feel inside, to fill it with something that makes us feel good in the moment.

> Pornography is the attempt to insult sex, to do dirt on it. —D. H. Lawrence

Pornography fills different needs for different people.

Some of you have never seen porn. Some of you look at it now and then, but you don't think it really affects you like it affects others. Some of you have a mild addiction, one that comes to the surface every few months. Some of you looked at porn last night and are apt to look at it again tonight after you close this book. Some of you are looking at it right now.

Certainly, you know the definition of porn: content that has the sole purpose of arousing the "God-given sexuality" in humans. But pornography has changed a lot in recent years. It's no longer simply pictures and movies. Unlike twenty years ago, today's content comes in more forms than just nudey magazines, bad seventies porn flicks, and gentlemen's clubs. Porn today has diversified. It can come in the form of chat rooms, forums, blogs, movies, website portals, books and stories, magazines, photographs, phone lines, live shows, advertising, and many other things.

Each pornographic form has a unique way of communicating sex. These communication techniques give pornography the opportunity to reach a wider audience with a message that speaks to an individual or group or demographic. This diversity and flexibility are a large part of why pornography has charmed its way into so many lives; it's the reason so many of us find it irresistible.

Here's another question.
I like questions, if you haven't noticed.

What need does porn fill in your life? In other words, what's missing [or unfulfilled] in your life that finds relief, satisfaction, or escape in pornography?

I believe many of us think that all we get from pornography is a quick, easy, and supposedly safe means to sexual arousal and gratification.

I don't believe this is true. Of course, generally the outcome of porn is sexual gratification. And although the self-induced orgasm feels good, it's not the *true* need we're trying to fill.

The different ways we experience, interact with, and become addicted to lust has changed since porn went DSL.

The invention of the Internet has, in my personal opinion, given a great deal of power and influence to pornography. The needs that the porn lifestyle can seemingly fill have widened drastically.

It's an understatement to suggest that porn has changed since it entered the Internet age in the early to midnineties. The obvious change is that it became available to a wider audience. Because of that availability, porn suddenly became every struggler's best [or worst] kept secret. Those who wanted to view it no longer had to smuggle a magazine into the house, sneak into a video store [and face the cashier], or venture out to a strip club [and risk seeing someone they knew]. All those who were once too scared to venture into this world suddenly got "brave." *Why?* Because the potential embarrassment of being seen [or caught] was taken out of the equation, we no longer had to worry about our reputations becoming tainted. Well, at least not publicly.

Fact: Porn Has a Price. Literally.

Billions of dollars get spent on porn each year. *That's insane.* Sure, there's plenty of free porn online or underneath your father's bed or at the neighbor's house. But eventually, if a person *really* wants to see and experience all that is available, this habit—whether big or small—ends up costing money. And face it: That's what the porn industry is banking on, that you'll come back and spend more. Sadly, some people get into financial trouble because of a porn habit. College students are often prone to put their porn on a Visa card. *Yikes!* Even more tragic, a lot of Internet porn addicts resist finding help because the help is often more expensive than their habit.

Another major difference the dot-com world has brought to porn is the difficulty the government has experienced in trying to enforce its "over eighteen" laws. As a result, many of you [lots of boys and some girls] hardly remember a time when porn wasn't a part of your life in some fashion. The creation of online porn has helped bring an already successful industry out of hiding. Today, pornography is one of the most successful facets of the entertainment industry — a 12 billion dollar a year industry and still growing. It makes more money than ABC, NBC, and CBS — *combined.*[12]

> Pornography is pornography, what is there to see? Movies are attempting to destroy something that's supposed to be the most beautiful thing a man and a woman can have by making it cheap and common. It's what you don't see that's attractive. — Nancy Reagan

The Internet has changed not only the availability of porn, the size of the industry, and porn's distribution to minors but also its role in the lives of those who download, chat, watch, read, and interact. Before the Internet, a person who wanted to actively interact with lust had to leave his or her home to do so. Experiencing porn through magazines and movies certainly made one feel lust, but the interaction that online porn allows people to experience — through chats, forums, cams, postings, and "live" shows — has indeed made a lot of people feel a connection to porn that didn't exist before the Internet.

This connection has made pornography more addictive, easier to hide, and much more difficult to bring under control.

The number of Christians who are closeted porn addicts is staggering.

Over e-mail, I communicated with a pastor who filled out my survey; he agreed to share a part of his story on the basis of anonymity.

"Back when I was teenager, the only porn I would see is pictures and poorly made X-rated movies," says a forty-year-old pastor from Maine who only recently has sought out help to combat a nine-and-a-half-year addiction to online pornography. "Honestly, the porn I witnessed in high school and in college was almost innocent compared to what's available online today.... But it wasn't simply the sexual release I craved; I was more addicted to the 'community' that I found through online porn. I had this crazy need to feel accepted and loved."

Recognize the needs people try to fill with pornography.

All of us have needs that we desire to have filled. Most of these needs are normal human feelings, but we have to be careful because it's easy to look in the wrong places for satisfaction. Some people use pornography to fill their needs. Here's a quick look at some of the desires porn can pretend to fill.

Pornography is far from harmless. It steals something from everyone it touches. Here are a few things porn can do in the life of an individual. For more information on the effects of pornography, visit XXXChurch.com.

Desensitizes you regarding sexual wrongdoing. Pornography can numb your ability to navigate through the right and wrong of your life. Whether you're married or single, by investing your head and heart into pornography, your capability to live holy and healthy in your relationships becomes crippled or paralyzed.

Alters how you view humanity. Pornography objectifies people. Lusting after the bodies and actions of real people will affect how you view your friends, family, and spouse or boyfriend or girlfriend. Some of you are reading this point and thinking this is crazy. But don't fool yourself; porn changes your perspective.

Ruins relationships. Pornography can ruin your relationship with the opposite sex. Marriages are broken because of porn. Dating relationships are severed. It's almost impossible for your habit not to affect the relationship you hold most dear.

Addiction is probable. Pornography teases and manipulates our senses, our emotions, our weaknesses, and our thinking. When those experiences get packaged inside a physical reaction [the orgasm], it creates an event that is highly addictive. Porn never satisfies. Instead, porn almost always makes you want to go to the next level. In most instances, it makes you want to experience another sexual high.

Pornography is a stepping-stone to other behavior. It's a proven fact that pornography, whether one is officially addicted or not, will lead you to do other things [like have sex with strangers, become an exhibitionist, create a sexual relationship online, become unhealthily connected to a fetish, and much worse].

Separates you from God. Although God never leaves your side, pornography, like other types of sin, keeps you from hearing Jesus speak to your heart.

Loneliness. Feeling lonely is a powerful emotion. Pornography can often make us feel a connection to strangers. Sometimes community is found around a particular fetish or sexual issue. Porn as a remedy for loneliness is only in our minds, but it still can be so powerful.

Personal insecurities. When people are online, they can become whomever they want. Whether it's being overweight, having insecurities about one's "look," or simply feeling socially awkward, these things can often drive us to begin living fake identities online or connect with others who feel similarly.

Relationships and community. Connection is one of the most powerful of all human needs. Everyone desires to feel close to people. If people don't have strong relationships or a community, it can often lead them to do drastic things in order to feel something. Looking at porn can falsely create this closeness. People with unhealthy minds believe that the feelings they experience when watching or interacting with pornography is the community they've desired all along.

This pastor from Maine knows the appeal well:

> Matthew,
> the hardest part of this struggle
> for me has been knowing that I have to let go of
> this whole other life that I have created over the last nine years
> online. I viewed the people I met inside sex chat rooms and on sex
> forums and at porn sites as friends. I kept in touch with them via a fake
> e-mail address. Sure, they didn't know what I looked like and they
> certainly didn't know my occupation, but still, I found so much peace
> and fulfillment knowing that this whole other world existed.
> Or at least, in my mind, it existed.

Depression or anxiety. Usually pornography can make depression or anxiety worse. The need to feel happy or calm doesn't ever get filled through porn, but a person's state of mind can be a path that leads to poor behavior. When they feel depressed, some people look for escape through porn.

Sexual arousal. Sometimes our bodies tell us we need to be touched, that we need to feel sexual closeness. *This is called being horny.* There are times when a person who is trying desperately to pursue holiness just feels horny. This state of mind can lead us to do some dumb stuff. Instead of prayerfully going to God with our desires, we go to the computer.

Story. We all want our personal story to be filled with mystery and excitement. For some, porn excites and mystifies more than anything else they experience. Sadly, it's easy for some people to let their entire life revolve around the feeling they get when they begin to view porn. If the excitement and mystery of their story is being defined by porn, there's a good chance they could be addicted.

Intimacy. For those who are not married or in a loving dating relationship, the desire for intimacy [touch, physical closeness, and the confidence that is gained through both] can be overwhelming. You'd be surprised how often pornography disguises itself as the real thing. This need can make some very good people do things that make themselves feel very dirty.

Boredom. Anyone who has found comfort in pornography will attest to boredom being a reason they sometimes stumble. Even the Bible talks about "idle hands" being a problem for some people.

The God-instilled need. In section 2, I talked about the need that God referred to when he said, "It's not good for man [or woman] to be alone." Sometimes people aren't aware how real and powerful this need can be in their lives. Like I said earlier, some try to fill this need with their career, wealth, or hobbies, and some try to fill it with sexual gratification through pornography.

There's more "connection" going on than you know.

Chatting with faceless people who like the same things they like can be a beautiful distraction for people in need. When they go online, they get the chance to leave their true existence behind for a time. Imagine the world they can create. A lovely, thirty-year-old woman who weighs 242 pounds can become HOTCHICK26 online. [This girl weighs 120 pounds and looks a little like Jennifer Garner.]

See the connection this kind of porn can bring into a person's life?

Renee's story:

I've been a Christian since I was six. My parents were missionaries in Kenya until I was sixteen. That's when we moved back to the States. Eventually, I went to a Christian college, got my degree in marketing, and moved to Orlando to begin working for a nonprofit ministry. Prior to that job, I had had only one boyfriend. We dated for seventeen months, but then he broke my heart when he cheated on me with a friend of mine at church. She was prettier than me. She was skinnier than me. She was more successful than me. Thankfully, I realized this guy's true colors before it was too late. But once I moved, I became a little depressed and felt lonely and displaced in my new surroundings. Instead of turning to family or friends or a church for help, I went online. Oh, it's not what you might think; I wasn't looking at pictures or watching movies or spending money on porn. Instead, I was going into free adult chat rooms and having intimate conversations with men from all over the world. The people I met online were kind, open to chatting about anything, and seemed like true friends. Almost anytime I wasn't working, I was online chatting with guys I didn't know. Every conversation started out the same way, just two people from two different places on the planet connecting via the Internet at one in the morning. Some of these guys were simply acquaintances. Some of these people became almost like secret boyfriends. Some of these people I would have cybersex with, sometimes phone sex.

The chat rooms became like a drug. On some days, I spent more than six hours talking. For three years, I lived this life. There were times when I would push away from family. I resisted getting connected in my church. I had very few lasting friendships or relationships. Online, I was pretty, sexy, charming, daring, sexual — everything I wasn't in real life.

Renee's story might sound insane, but it's more common than you might think. She wasn't looking at pictures of naked men; she was pretending to have sex with random guys all over the world. She had no idea what they looked like, how old they were, or where they were from. She was in a way becoming these guys' personal "porn" story. Eventually, Renee's depression led her into counseling, where she confessed her secret life. But it took months of counseling before she was able to see that her fake life was indeed an addiction that needed to be broken. She has since found healing.

Pornography can turn you into something you never thought you'd become. It can make you live a life that for a time feels amazing but eventually leaves you feeling empty, shameful, and devastated. But despite the emptiness you feel, you go back to it hoping another hint of satisfaction will help make the feelings go away.

This probably won't surprise you, but every guy except one who filled out my survey confessed that porn was, in some way, a part of his life. Sixty-two percent of the women confessed the same. Here are some of their responses. To protect their identity, all names have been changed:

▶ "I've been in 'recovery' for more than two years. Some weeks, I spend twenty hours or more looking at pornography." —*Jansen, 28*

▶ "Looking at porn makes me feel like I'm the most disgusting human being on the planet, and yet, at least two or three times a month, I'm online." —*William, 23*

▶ "When I was eighteen, I bought a cam. I met a guy in an online Christian forum once. We chatted for months. I didn't tell anyone about him. He didn't tell anyone about me. Some nights we would strip for each other on cam." —*Brea, 23*

▶ "I've only looked at porn four or five times in my life, but whenever I am tempted to masturbate, it's often those images that come to mind." —*Ben, 21*

▶ "No one knows that I'm addicted to porn. I've looked at it almost every day for two years. My girlfriend has no clue. I've almost become numb to it now; it's a part of my life's routine. I've tried to stop on a couple of occasions but haven't stopped yet." —*Johnson, 26*

▶ "I look at porn. One of my ex-boyfriends [before I was

a Christian] got me into it. We'd use it to better our sex lives. We've been broken up for four years. I don't look at it every day, not even every week, but at least once a month."
—*Natalie, 29*

♥♥♥

Lust is a hideous word. It's not just the meaning of the word that makes it so ugly to me. It's also the sound that *L, U, S,* and *T* make when put together in that order.

Anything can make an individual feel lust. Words do it. Pictures do it. Sounds do it. We don't have to be told when to lust. We just need a thought to be led there. Once our interest is piqued, the thought of turning away becomes more difficult to accomplish. Of course, lust isn't just a sex thing. You can feel lust for almost anything—money, power, success, sex, and freedom are among the most popular.

For the follower of Jesus, I think David might have said it best when he wrote these words:

[God], don't let me lust for evil things;
  don't let me participate in acts of wickedness.
Don't let me share in the delicacies
  of those who do evil. (Psalm 141:4, NLT)

Do you have a secret life you're afraid to let anyone know about? Is it porn? Is it cybersex inside chat rooms? Is it strip clubs? Are you having sex with strangers? Is it simply one or two pictures you keep in a hidden file on your computer?

I know what some of you are feeling. I haven't had sex with strangers and I've never gone to a strip club, but I've had a problem with online porn. I want you to know this: You're not weird or gross. You're not a lesser human being because of your struggle. And, oh yeah, you're not alone.

I'm not a preacher-like individual who is trying to make you live a certain way or feel guilty about what you do. I don't believe guilt helps in this struggle. But I do know a little about what you're feeling, what you're going through behind closed doors. And I know the idea of "coming clean" with what's happening in your life is scary. It was scary for me, too. For some of you, it feels like your world might fall apart if anyone ever found out the "true" you.

But have you considered the idea that your life might fall apart if you don't seek help?

It happens that way all the time. But no matter how deep in it you might feel, hope and healing do exist for you.

BUT . . . [and I hate that word]

You first have to admit what's going on in your life. You have to be honest with yourself. You have to be honest with someone else. You have to get help.

Some Help For You

[because the last sentence in that last paragraph is true — more than you know]

The following is a list of ideas that many people find helpful on the road to walking away from pornography. Every person's experience is different. These are not rules. These are suggestions. When I was in the middle of my struggle, the last thing I wanted to hear was a bunch of rules. But deep down, I also craved help.

☻ Be honest with yourself about the pornography that exists in your life. Be honest about its effects on your life. Be honest about the need [or needs] it's filling.

☻ Identify what you're feeling when you find yourself desiring to experience porn. Is it boredom? Is it loneliness? Is it the need for relationships? Is it quick sexual gratification? It's helpful to spend time thinking about the deficiencies in your life that make you gravitate toward pornography.

☻ Talk to someone you trust. This might be a friend, an old youth pastor, your dad, or a counselor. This probably won't be the only person you'll have to tell, but getting your struggle out on the table with someone you trust will help you gain strength.

☻ Make drastic decisions about habits if necessary. Often people try to stop their habit many times before they're successful. But sometimes success requires drastic measures. This might include installing a porn filter on your computer or getting rid of the Internet in your house or moving your computer into a room where other people always are or never being alone in the house. This also might mean seeking out counseling. Sure, some of these tactics might seem a bit over the top; you're right, they are over the top. But so is being completely naked at your computer at four in the morning looking at naked women with your hand in your crotch.

☻ Ask a friend [a same-sex friend] if he or she would be an accountability partner for you in your recovery. Sometimes simply having an individual in your life who is willing to ask you "how you're doing" will help you remain focused — not perfect, but focused.

☻ If your problem persists or you feel you're addicted, you need to seek professional help. More than likely this problem will not be rectified through simple actions. Visit www.sa.org for more information about getting help, or ask your church counselor if he or she offers help with sexually related issues.

☻ Jesus LOVES you more than you will ever understand. Know this to be true throughout your journey toward a holy and healthy sexual lifestyle.

☻ Remember, you might feel like pornography is defining your spiritual life, but if you're alive in Christ, Jesus says it is not. His blood is powerful enough to cover what you're feeling inside.

OKAY, IF EVERYTHING ELSE FAILS, THIS IS MY LAST IDEA, AND IT'S A LITTLE OUT THERE.

As you probably know, temptation sometimes arises when you're all by yourself. If this should occur, follow these instructions:

1. Find a picture of your mom.
2. Stare at it for three minutes.
3. Think about what she would feel if she knew what you were doing.
4. Picture her brow turned downward, her nostrils flaring, and her eyes full of horror and shame—all because of what you're doing.
5. Think about the sorrow you would hear in her voice over what you're doing.
6. You should now be hearing your mother's voice saying, *Tommy,* I love you. Tommy, I raised you the best way I could. Tommy, please step away from that computer and put your hands to your sides.*
7. E-mail me if this works.

---

* Of course, insert your own name here.

Some of you reading this have no idea what it's like to suffer from a porn problem. You might have experienced porn before, but you found the material disgusting to your spirit. So you're not drawn to it. It's not a temptation. If this is you, you might be able to help those who do walk this crazy road. Here are some guidelines that might help you see [and understand] the part you can play in helping others recover. [If you're a girl, you should resist trying to help a guy. And vice versa.]

Offer a safe environment. People who desire to recover need a safe place to confess or get things off their minds. Be a safe place for your friends to come and share what's on their hearts. When they open up about their struggle, resist the urge to judge or to act completely shocked by their actions.

Help them be accountable. If you're truly not tempted by porn or other types of sexual sin, you are the best kind of accountability partner to those who are going through it. Too often people who are keeping each other accountable don't end up helping each other; their mutual problem can often create an opportunity for more failure.

Be a support through prayer. Porn addicts [or those who find porn fascinating] need your emotional and mental support, but they also need you to be praying for them.

Challenge them. If friends struggling with porn come to you with this problem and ask for your help, make sure they know that sometimes you're going to have to be tough with them, that you feel it's your responsibility to gracefully [yet consistently] point them back toward Jesus and what he ultimately desires.

What NOT to do is just as important as what you SHOULD do.

Do not judge ever. Usually people who struggle with porn are already feeling enough judgment and condemnation [from within or from an outside source]; they do not need you to add to those feelings. If they are openly seeking help, you can be sure they already know that what they're doing is wrong. They simply need someone to lean on.

Resist trying to SAVE them. It's *not* your responsibility to save your friends from their addiction. That would be codependence. Create healthy boundaries at the beginning such as a particular time set aside for talking, how late

Even the Apostle Paul Would Appreciate These "Porn" Sites.

☒ **XXXChurch.com.** This website is perhaps the coolest and most popular of all the Christian antiporn sites. Its best feature is the accountability software called X3. This free download is designed to record every website you visit, create a report, and send it to the accountability person of your choice via e-mail. This is a great way for you and a friend to monitor each other's Internet activity. The only downfall of XXXChurch.com is that it's sometimes difficult to decipher the important information from some of the fluffier stuff on the site [*kind of like this book*]. **RATING: 8 out of 10 [practical, fun, community]**

☒ **PureOnline.com.** Everything about this site is great except its motto—*30 days to purity*. To me, purity of heart and mind has a lot more to it than simply whether or not one is looking at porn. But besides that, PureOnline.com offers online seminars that give you basic instructions on how to overcome the stronghold of porn in your life. It offers online programs and counseling for those who are single and for those who are married. But be aware: At PureOnline.com, there's a financial cost involved to becoming pure in thirty days! **RATING: 6.5 out of 10 [concise, creative, but pricey]**

he or she can contact you, and so on. Remember, good boundaries are not simply for your benefit but also for the benefit of others.

Don't preach at them. If you're a "preacher," you aren't helping. You can offer advice, but do not act like you know everything about their addiction because you don't know what they're feeling. So resist the urge to constantly give advice. In fact, a good rule of thumb is to offer your words only when they are solicited.[13]

What You Didn't Learn from Your Parents About Sex Presents:
Answers to *a Whole Bunch* of Your Most Intriguing Sex Questions!

We, the editors of *What You Didn't Learn from Your Parents About Sex,* are rather crazy individuals. [We're crazy like Kanye West is full of himself.] And so far in this book, we've had it rather easy. So we've decided Matthew deserves a break since he just finished writing a very LONG section about a very difficult topic. And when we say long, we mean L-O-N-G. And when we say difficult, we mean BALANCE BEAM difficult. We have no clue how those little Olympians stay on that beam. So please don't ask us that question. And since it's impossible to cover *every* one of your issues and questions [*some of you have a lot of them*] in as concise a manner as Matthew has the topics of masturbation and pornography [and he's got more to cover later on in this section], we thought we would come alongside him and get a little crazy with a marathon run of answering four of your most intriguing questions all in one session.

▢ **Porn-Free.org.** Offering literary teaching on all the various forms of sexual addiction, Porn-Free.org is a not-for-profit ministry whose thought process focuses on basic Bible principles. Although its tactics and teachings do lean a little toward the charismatic side [and at times come across a little harsh], this website, though not extremely cool, does cover topics in a concise and thorough manner. **RATING: 5 out of 10 [strict, but information on almost *everything* is available]**

▢ **FiresOfDarkness.com.** *The name says it all. Wow.* But the apostle Paul might still like it, and despite a lot of its content coming from Porn-Free .org, it does a better job at categorizing its information. **RATING: 3 out of 10 [the name *Fires of Darkness* is just a wee bit dramatic]**

Other Sites You Might Want to Visit

⊞ No-Porn.com
⊞ PureWarrior.com
⊞ SexHelp4Porn.com
⊞ AvenueResource.com

So let's get right to the first question.

1. QUESTION: Dear editors, every time my boyfriend and I make out, he gets up right in the middle of our time and practically runs out of my apartment, mumbling, "I need to go, baby; I need to go." Do you have any idea what's going on? — Molly, 19 [almost 20!]

ANSWER: Hey, Molly dear! Thanks a lot for e-mailing us your question. Your boyfriend sounds like a real gem. You see, baby, when you and your man are busy being *intimate [you know, kissing and stuff]*, he will often get what is called an erection. This happens when the spongelike tissue inside a man's penis becomes filled up with blood and becomes hardened. A guy can get an erection for various reasons: gusty breezes, nervousness, stretching, holding your hand, kissing, and, of course, any kind of sexual contact. However, just because your boyfriend gets an erection while holding your hand [and it doesn't always happen], this doesn't mean he's a pervert or lusting. It just might be he's nervous, we mean, *normal*. This is how God made men.

Now to explain why he's *getting up* and leaving the room. He's doing this because he respects you, Molly, and he doesn't want to put the two of you in a compromising position. He knows his limits and apparently doesn't know yours.

If we were you — but of course we're not — we'd keep him! *Tootles!*

2. QUESTION: Dear editors, my girlfriend and I want to know if oral sex before marriage is wrong. — Derek, 24

ANSWER: Derek, you've asked a question that a lot of Christians are wondering these days. Here's the deal: The Bible does not mention oral sex by name. So we can't be sure exactly what God's thinking on the topic is. Most assume, as do we, that within marriage, oral sex is a wonderful thing. And considering that we're married, you can believe us when we say it is indeed a wonderful thing.

However, God deems the pursuit of holiness extremely crucial within relationships, whether married or dating. And he does say that all sexual intimacy should be saved for marriage. You'd agree that oral sex is sexually intimate, yes? So we the editors believe that oral sex should be reserved for marriage. It comes down to the fact that oral sex initiates an orgasm between two people. *And now, our dismount:* We believe God has reserved such intimacy for a husband and wife, and Derek, you should wait to unleash the *oral passion* when you and your girl are under the marriage covenant.

We have spoken!
Tootles!

3. QUESTION: Dear editors, my best friend just got married. And now he claims that God has bestowed upon him a "new spiritual gift." Can you please tell me if it's sacrilegious to say that God would give the spiritual gift of sex? — Kenny, 22

ANSWER: Oh, Kenny, how exciting for your friend that he's been given the "gift of tongues: the remixed version." All we got was discernment.

Here's the deal: We don't think it's necessarily irreverent of your friend to refer to his married sexual prowess as a spiritual gift. In fact, we think it's downright hilarious, and his wife probably LOVES his newly discovered gift. Of course, if he goes overboard with describing his gift, you should certainly tell him to keep his married relationship private.

However, Kenny, as long as he's not oversharing, we think you should be excited for your friend, and when [or if] you get married, you should totally claim that God has given you the power to "part the Jordan River with your staff."

We're not sure this makes one lick of sense, but it will make your friend think!

Always remember: Before you get in the sack, have a marriage contract!

Tootles.

4. QUESTION: Dear editors, I'm a virgin, but my boyfriend is not. As we get closer to marriage, I'm having a lot of trouble knowing how to handle my boyfriend's nonpure state. Can this relationship work? — Bethany, 26

ANSWER: Greetings, Bethany! We get this question a lot! And it's a tricky one to answer without knowing a couple's situation. But we're gonna do our best to point you in a good direction, baby. But know that depending on how troubled you are over this, counseling might be in order.

First off, let's answer your last question: Can this relationship work? Absolutely. But it depends on the two of you working through this together. Here are a few things to consider.

How active has your man been? Are we talking Danny Bonaduce active [which is very active]? Or are we talking one or two partners active? Either way, you first want to make sure he gets tested for STDs; you certainly don't want to deal with any surprises after you're engaged and preparing for the married life. You will also want to be sure that this activity isn't part of a deeper behavioral issue your man is dealing with. In other words, does he have sex-addiction tendencies? Does he have issues with commitment? If so, has he dealt with these issues? Was he a Christian when this activity happened? The answers to these questions are important to know before you can begin to deal with your insecurities about your relationship.

What's the root issue here for you? Bethany, knowing exactly why you're feeling the way you do will be important as you and your boyfriend work through this issue. Are you insecure about him potentially making performance comparisons to his past lovers? Are you simply upset because you always wanted to marry a virgin? Is your frustration family related? All of these issues are understandable. But before you can come to a conclusion, you need to ask God to reveal to you why you're having these feelings.

And lastly, are you both willing to work through this? Is your man patient enough to work through this? Are you flexible enough to possibly change how you're thinking about this relationship? Do you both believe it's worth it? If the answer is yes to these questions, then you should seek out wise counsel from a pastor, mentor, or professional therapist and begin to work through this issue with someone you trust. A counselor will help you navigate your way through all of your questions, your lover's past, and the future that God can create for you.

Don't fret too much, B! You'll get through this!

Tootles!

>>The editors

PS: Send us your questions at WeLoveWritingForMatthew@ yahoo.com.

Other Sex Stuff You Need to Know
[or at least need to think about]

Sexually transmitted diseases don't skip Christians.

Even if you're not sexually active, most statistics suggest that 50 percent of nonmarried Christians are. So don't be naive. Just in case you begin dating one of the "touched" 50 percent from your church's singles' group, knowledge about STDs could be extremely important [and asking those hard questions might just save your life]. What many Christians might not know is that the U.S. has one of the highest STD rates in the world. Find out more information at http://www.ashastd.org/.

Consider these frightening statistics:

- One in five Americans has an STD.
- Eighty percent of Americans infected with genital herpes don't know it.
- Sixty-six percent of STD cases in the United States are individuals under age twenty-five.
- Fifteen percent of female infertility comes from tubal damage caused by pelvic inflammatory disease, the result of an untreated STD.[14]

Don't have "friends with benefits."

Some of you are like, *I would never do that!* And others of you are thinking, *Been there, done that!* And a few of you are wondering, *What is that?*

An FWB [friend with benefits] is a friendship between two people who have an assumed "mutual agreement" to offer one another physical favors with no "relationship/commitment" [*you know, the stuff that gets in the way of sex*] in return. Not all of these agreements involve sex; sometimes the benefits include only kissing and fondling. But no matter what the terms of the contract are, this kind of friendship is stupid, is not what God has in mind for his followers, and ALWAYS ends up being more than what you bargained for.

Girls often have FWBs because: "Let's face it: There are a lot of sexually frustrated people out there," says Jen, a thirty-something Christian single who has experience being a friend with benefits. "It's easy just to fill that need with whatever is available. So because I was feeling lonely and maybe a little insecure, I simply invested a part of myself into a 'friendship' and ended up getting bit in the a%$."

Guys often have FWBs because: "It's always about the benefits," says Tucker, a twenty-six-year-old chemist who during college had three different "friendships." "When guys go into these kinds of relationships, it's all about them and never about the other person. They're looking to get some action for nothing in return."

But the truth is: This kind of relationship is not only stupid and less than God's best for your life, but it's also a complete farce. Somebody always ends up feeling things that are not written in the contract. Both guys and girls can end up making this mistake, but often it's the girl who ends up losing much more than the guy.

Sexual abuse will follow you.

Sexual abuse comes in many different forms—rape, pedophilia, harassment, unwelcome advances, spiritually infused abuse, and the list goes on. Sexual abuse affects its victims in a number of ways. But one thing is usually certain: It does affect you.

We live in a time when it's very likely that you or someone you know has been sexually abused. It's a topic that the media has been covering extensively for some time. But most of the time, we hear only a small fraction of the story. Despite the attention this issue receives today, many people are still fearful about sharing their stories and pursuing the help they need to live fulfilling lives. Men and women from all walks of life [including a vast majority of Christians] are attempting to trek through this dark battle alone, without the community of support and hope they need to mentally, emotionally, and spiritually survive.

This topic is much too delicate to handle tritely in a book such as this one. My only reason for mentioning it is this: Sexual abuse—whether physical, mental, emotional, or spiritual—affects a person's ability to live a holy and healthy sexual lifestyle. Sometimes it's the healthy part people struggle with; sometimes it's the holy. No matter what the situation was, how long ago it happened, or how well you believe you're dealing with it now, abuse, if not handled with care, counseling, and courage, will almost always come to the surface within the context of a dating or marriage relationship. It might happen tomorrow; it might happen twenty years from now. But it will happen.

Resist the urge to just let it slide. Talk about it. Get help. If you haven't shared your story with your spouse or significant other, you might consider talking with a counselor or therapist to see if he or she recommends that you should. Just don't be silent.

This might surprise you, but I am not a sexual abuse expert. You're shocked, huh? Yeah, right. Well, because I'm not an expert, I interviewed someone who is. His name is Mark Bonham, and he's the executive director for Open Hearts Ministry. I'll let him explain his ministry, but pay close attention to the wisdom he gives regarding the effects and healing of sexual abuse.

MPT: Will you please tell me a little about Open Hearts Ministry?

MARK: Open Hearts Ministry (OHM) trains leaders to facilitate "Grace Groups." Grace Groups typically have six participants with two leaders and focus on soul wounds of all kinds [sexual, physical, emotional, and spiritual, as well as abandonment and neglect]. Open Hearts has trained leaders in over forty states and twenty-six countries. Grace Groups accompany people on their journey of recovery, using a twelve- or twenty-four-week curriculum published by OHM. Training occurs during a six-day seminar called SALTS (Survivors of Abuse Leadership Training Seminar), which is held at various times and places around the world. Contact OHM for more information: 161 E. Michigan Ave., Suite 600, Kalamazoo, MI 49007; telephone: 269-383-3597; e-mail: office@ohmin. org; website: www.ohmin.org.

MPT: Can a person recover from sexual abuse without assistance?

MARK: Because sexual abuse is relational betrayal, it does damage to relationships. For that reason, healing from sexual abuse best occurs in safe relationships. Since sexual abuse typically carries huge amounts of shame, relationships are impacted. People in shame tend to hide. Poor responses to the disclosure of abuse have led to more shame. Dealing with shame requires stepping into the light with people who can affirm dignity without patronizing and expose depravity without shaming.

MPT: How can hidden sexual abuse play out in one's marriage?

MARK: Sexual abuse impacts the sexual identity of men and women. The list of ways this can occur is long. Here are just a few examples: (1) inhibited sexual desire; (2) flashbacks during sex; (3) fear of intimacy [feels invasive]; (4) sexual identity confusion; (5) perversion of male strength or female beauty; (6) emotional deadness and ambivalence; (7) sexual control; (8) selective impotence; (9) poor body image; (10) inappropriate emotional responses, ranging from angry outbursts to numbness.

MPT: For people who have not dealt with their abuse, how do you recommend they begin that process?

MARK: Victims of abuse need a safe place to tell their story. They need someone who can cover their shame with grace, validate their pain with empathy, and affirm their dignity with truth. Finding a good counselor would be a place to start. But wounded people benefit greatly when they know they are not alone, when they can see others who are moving toward recovery, and when they can begin to have hope that stories of abuse can be redeemed. This occurs best in safe groups that understand this process. Silence compounds shame. People in pain need to talk. The question is, will there be someone who can listen?

Celibacy is a true calling.

My personal opinion about God's calling an individual to live without sex for a lifetime drastically changed after my wife introduced me to a friend of hers who is currently pursuing his call to the priesthood.

Before I met Dan Schuster, the idea of celibacy seemed about as far-fetched as the special effects in a *Left Behind* movie. But a conversation with him last year gave me a new perspective about celibacy that I [perhaps naively] had never considered. For the first time, I listened to a man explain his pursuit of a nonsexual, chaste lifestyle as a calling rather than a gift. I'm not sure why, but I could never get my heart and soul around calling celibacy a gift. But a God-given calling, maybe because it seems more humanly comprehendible, I could grasp.

"It's not like I never feel sexual, man," Dan admitted, talking to me over the phone from his seminary outside of

Chicago. "But I know I'm called to this higher way of living life for a purpose. It's not higher as in better than the life you're living, Matthew. But it is a better life for me because it's based on God asking me to make a sacrifice."

To listen to this young man, a regular guy who likes football, beer, and rock 'n' roll, most would never look at him and think "priest." But to hear him talk of his calling is like listening to a child talk about his first trip to the ocean: full of wonder, anticipation, and conviction. At times, as I listened to the passion in his voice, I would forget that he was talking about pursuing a life that will require him to live without experiencing the sexual love of a woman.

For many Christians, myself included, the very thought of sacrificing something so amazing is uncanny. But that's okay. It's not our calling.

When Dan began feeling the reality of his calling, he was on the verge of marrying his high school sweetheart. He explained, "When I first thought about this calling, I had my doubts. I knew how big this decision would be for me and also for my family."

With Matthew 19:12 as his creed—"Some are born as eunuchs, some have been made that way by others, and some choose not to marry for the sake of the Kingdom of Heaven"

(NLT)—Dan desires that his life will advance the kingdom. "I'm called to give my life away to people in need; that's what I want my life to be about. I firmly believe God has ordained marriage for his good, but I believe wholeheartedly that I am called to give away a part of my life for what I know will be a much sweeter return."

I asked Dan this question: "If in the next ten years, the Catholic Church were to allow priests to marry, would that change your calling?" He thought about it for a second and then, quite emphatically, said, "No."

For more information about the Catholic Church's theological thinking behind celibacy, visit MonksOfAdoration.org/conslife.html.

Unmarried Intimacy — Is It a Myth?

Usually when one considers an unmarried couple's physical activity, the question often asked is this one: How far is too far? Of course, there's this one, too: Where should I draw the line?

Let me guess. You've asked one of these questions before, right? Most of us have.

However, I've come to hate these kinds of questions. They might be suitable inquiries if one is in high school or just entering his or her college career, but for someone who is pursuing a lasting and potentially lifelong relationship with the opposite sex, I think these questions have either little significance or far too much.

Every answer I have heard people give in reference to these kinds of questions either reeks of legalism or has no biblical value whatsoever. Physical intimacy before marriage between two people who love each other isn't supposed to be bridled by rules or without a holy foundation.

In my opinion, unmarried intimacy can't be defined with rigid lines that dictate what is permissible and what is not. Are there guidelines and biblical concepts one can/should follow? Sure. But there is not a definition, an exact answer, to the question "how far is too far?"

If one believes the Bible to be the inspired Word of God, then one must also believe that God is speaking to us through the stories, quotes, and lifestyles of those included. Had God wanted to draw distinct, rigid lines around the permissible physical intimacy one should share before marriage, I'm pretty sure he would have spelled out precisely the line over which one goes from being completely pure to utterly abominable.

In other words, if kissing were the line [and I'm not saying it is or isn't], wouldn't God have communicated that in

Scripture? I mean, he does get quite specific, especially in the Old Testament. In Leviticus alone, we read how God is not fond of everything from a person wearing multifabric clothing to the mixed grazing of cattle to his intolerance of blind people bringing food to his altar.

God seems pretty detailed in Scripture. If premarital kissing leaves such a bad taste in God's mouth, I believe he would have made the line clear. But I don't find that "line" in Scripture.

However, a lot of Christians believe he does define that line.

Things get very complicated when Christians create their own lines deeming what God does and does not find appropriate before marriage.

I have spent many hours scouring the Internet looking for Christians' opinions and thoughts on this topic. And you might be happy to learn that a lot of people know exactly what you and your significant other should — *and should not* — be doing before you get hitched. Sometimes the advice of people is a bit over the top. One blogger's advice? "Don't be fooled, Christians; hand holding leads to babies!" *Hand holding leads to babies? I don't even know how to think about that.*

Most comments aren't that extreme. But a few do get rather interesting.

In my research, I came across an organization named Probe Ministries. Yes, the ministry is called *Probe*. [To comment further would be way too easy.] This not-for-profit's goal is to equip the church and world with sound biblical information. When it comes to their opinion about "unmarried intimacy," the perspective is quite conservative. In reference to the question "how far is too far?" Sue, a speaker and frequent contributor to Probe's online content, answered this way: You shouldn't touch the opposite sex "in a way you wouldn't dream of touching one's pastor [or pastor's wife, depending on your gender]." *This struck me as weird. The only thing I would ever offer my pastor is a handshake, maybe a hug on a special occasion. I don't think I have ever touched his wife.* But Sue backs her logic up with 1 Corinthians 7:1: "It is good for a man not to touch a woman" (KJV). [*Between you and me, she's taking this out of context.*]

But alas, it was Sue's "dismount" that really got me thinking. She concluded that the "line" comes down to this: "I suggest that 'the line' be drawn somewhere between a short kiss and a long kiss. Short kisses are not sexual, but long kisses are. Sexual arousal happens after you cross the line from a short kiss to a long kiss."

What do Sue's words mean for you? I'm not exactly sure, but I believe a stopwatch might help you figure that out.

In an article called "Principles for Dating," written by a respected Bible teacher named Patrick, his message was similar to Probe's, but his illustration was a bit different. "When asked, 'How far is too far?'" wrote Patrick, "I respond to the guys, 'How far would you go with your own sister?' To the girls I say, 'How far would you go with your own brother?'"

He goes on to say that relationships should be built on righteousness [very true], but he stops short of pointing out what he believes is the ideal line you should never cross. Yet if you consider his whole "brother/sister" logic, his view might be more conservative than Sue's. Think about it: In America, we might hug our brothers and sisters, perhaps kiss them on the cheek, but very few of us kiss our siblings on the lips. [*Well, some states bend that rule a bit.*] So while Sue thinks short kisses are fine, Patrick might believe couples should give only short "good-bye-like" hugs.

Some of you might believe these examples to be extreme and perhaps illogical, but these perspectives are not that uncommon within the culture of Christianity. Consider these exact quotes from ministries and Christian bloggers in answering the question "how far is too far?"

SilverRingThing.com, a Christian teen advice site, answers this way: "Think of a car. Everything in it is built so that it can move. It wasn't built just to sit in your driveway. It was built to travel. But it can't move until you put the key in the ignition and start the engine. However, you can't drive unless you have a license. Right? If you don't have your license or a permit, you are not going anywhere. There is a right time for you to drive." You know where he's going with this, right? Yeah, I thought so.

Twentysomething Jason at RustyParts.com has a "sexual ethics" page where Christian couples can find out his thoughts on the BIG question: "My youth pastor's advice was 'don't do anything you would be uncomfortable doing in front of your parents.' However, I feel pretty uncomfortable just holding hands in front of my mom. . . . [So] I have limited it to kissing (without too much intimacy)."

ByFaith.co.uk says, "If you have decided not to be controlled by lust, you'll know to keep your

Just One More Reason to Not Have Sex Before You're Hitched

FACT: Okay, so here's an interesting fact: The average healthy man, according to the World Health Organization, emits 40,000,000 sperm in one ejaculation. FORTY MILLION! Of course, not all of the sperm are completely functional. But still, one shot could potentially have enough dosage to "help" procreate a group of people the population of New York City.

hands to yourself. Touching people sexually inevitably leads to something deeper."

▸▸ **SoulPurpose.co.nz** encourages the youth and young adults of New Zealand to follow this rule: "If you can't do it in front of your parents, then you shouldn't be doing it at all!"

▸▸ **The folks at IntoTheLight.org** answer like this: "Remember, what you do will affect the rest of your life. Is it really that important to have a boyfriend? Fifteen minutes of pleasure vs. an eternity in a flaming inferno called hell. The choice is yours!" I have one question: What teenage boy could go fifteen minutes?

▸▸ **TheBibleIsTrue.com** is frank: "If a guy is touching the breast of anyone he is not married to, he is embracing the bosom of another man's wife (adultery), whether or not she is currently married." *Wow!*

▸▸ **The apostle Paul** might answer the question like this: "Our bodies were not made for sexual immorality. They were made for the Lord, and the Lord cares about our bodies. . . . Run away from sexual sin! No other sin so clearly affects the body as this one does. For sexual immorality is a sin against your own body" (1 Corinthians 6:13,18, NLT).

But no matter what other Christians think about the physical aspects of dating, if you want to lead a holy and healthy sexual life, you have to come to terms with how you think about this issue, how your history has affected your thinking, and the motives of your heart.

Questions to Consider When Thinking About Unmarried Intimacy

The following questions are not all biblically based. Some of them are simply based on common sense or the lessons our culture has learned about the human psyche. Of course, when you're "in love," many times common sense and a healthy human psyche are the first things to go. *You probably know what I'm talking about.* But I believe these questions will help you make wise decisions when thinking about the physical aspect of your dating relationships. Well, they will if you're into Oprah-type thinking. If not, you'll roll your eyes and think derogatory thoughts about me. And that's okay. But read them anyway.

? **Is the relationship worth pursuing?** Holy and healthy living requires you to ponder the seriousness of your relationship. Would you consider marrying the person you're dating? Are you at an age or a place in your personal life where you're prepared to even consider marriage an option? Once you've answered those questions in the affirmative, ask this one: Do both you and your "lover" feel the same? Holy intimacy—which includes the physical, emotional, and spiritual aspects — must be built on truth, love, and passion. If you're the least bit unsure about your relationship, the last thing you should be thinking about is pursuing intimacy of any kind, whether it be kissing or something considered more passionate. True intimacy is always a product of real feelings, feelings shared by both people and built on how God defines love in 1 Corinthians 13. If you're pursuing intimacy with someone you barely know or someone who is obviously "not your type," your feelings are developing out of unhealthy emotion or need. *I hate being blunt, but it might only be lust that you're feeling.* Yes, these relationships happen, but they *only* lead to pain. If there is no future in the relationship, then you shouldn't even consider physical intimacy.

? **Are your motives pure?** Many times when a Christian involves himself or herself in an unholy physical relationship, self-pleasure is the main motive. That's why it's important to assess your objectives for being in your current relationship or your desires for becoming physical. Are your feelings to touch and be intimate with your boyfriend or girlfriend an overflow of love and appreciation, or are they based on a desire to see how far you can go? In other words, are you being selfless or selfish?

? **Have you talked to each other about your personal boundaries?** Discussing each other's values and personal convictions is crucial in the journey of holy intimacy. If you've never thought about your personal physical boundaries, you need to do that. Make sure you think about your boundaries in light of both God's teaching and what he's communicating to your soul. Resist the temptation to simply take on the guidelines and rules of someone else. Someone else's values won't hold true for you unless you know and experience the depth of their meaning. That's why it's of utmost importance for each of us to consider for ourselves what Jesus holds for us. Perhaps most important is making sure you're willing to respect and hold to the values that the other feels are important. In a relationship, the most important facet is your willingness to serve the other. This ability to serve should flow out of your love for Christ, not out of selfishness or self-fulfillment.

? **What mistakes have you made in the past?** This one is important. Let's face it: A lot of us have made mistakes in the past that have proven pretty devastating to our minds and hearts, not to mention to the relationships we were pursuing. If you've been sexually active in the past or are consumed with guilt because from your perspective you've "gone too far," before moving forward you need to heal, identify what God deems important, and dig into the reasons that led you to jump the gun on God's plan for your life. The worst thing you can do is enter another relationship still broken from the past. Sure, we're never going to have it all together, but a heart that is passionately pursuing the things God deems holy and healthy will be better prepared to not allow past brokenness to play itself out again in future relationships.

? **Is Jesus your center?** Rules and other people's theories cannot be the foundations for what we do and do not do in relationships. *They don't hold true.* All of us are incapable of making right choices without Jesus being the center of our being. This won't mean you'll be perfect, but with Jesus at the center of your life, you'll be more apt to dive into embracing humility, servanthood, and selflessness in a relationship with the opposite sex. That's the kind of life that radiates holy and healthy intimacy before and after marriage. That's the life we're called to live.

Learning to Ask the Right Questions

I met a gorgeous girl named Jennifer at a Christian music concert. Any relationship that begins with praise-and-worship music can't be all bad, right? *Little did I know.*

The event was at Jammin Java, the faith-based coffeehouse I managed, and the room was packed with people that night. When Jennifer walked through the front doors with a couple of her friends [one of which I knew], I experienced a moment. You know, like the feeling people get when they think they've encountered an angel.

Because of the hustle and bustle happening in the room, I had not noticed her until her hand grazed mine as she handed me her ticket. Still not looking, I ripped her ticket in half, looked up to hand back her half, and suddenly the room stopped.

>>[Okay, stop for a moment; I need to explain something here. Of course, the "room stopping" description is a literary exaggeration; in the writing world we call this kind of phrase a hyperbole. I just don't want you to think that the room really stopped; it didn't. But saying it did does paint a nice picture, doesn't it? Okay, back to the story. **This next part is very dramatic.**]<<

In a moment's glance, Jennifer's presence—her glowing smile, the sweetness of her voice, her hot body—permeated every sensory organ I knew existed within my body, and also a few I didn't know I had. It was the kind of moment when you feel like you should look up into the heavens and just thank God to be alive. Sadly, I couldn't help but do all the stupid things that average-looking twentysomething guys do when they're graced by the presence of a woman they assume is out of their league. My voice cracked. The hugeness of my smile made me seem much too eager. My mannerisms shouted overcompensation. And the first words that came out of my mouth were pretty much incoherent.

Of course, she made no mistakes.

Since she worked in Washington, D.C., and was a professionally trained communicator, her ability to convey her thoughts was flawless. Her words even smelled good as they popped out of her mouth and into my ears [and nostrils]. The guy who was with her [the one I knew] introduced us.

[All of that happened in like thirty seconds — *maybe forty-five.* But it was quick.]

Despite my first impression being short and coming off like a forced sequel to a bad movie, I was shocked when Jennifer called me the very next day and asked me out to dinner; she wanted to talk business. *Yeah, right.* Over Thai food and better conversation, I put on the best *Christian* act I could muster up. And of course, having been raised Baptist, I was a natural. She did the same, and she was equally as good. That night, while talking business, a connection ensued. I'm not sure if it was simply physical attraction that drew us together — because she was hot, beauty queen hot — or if a true spiritual, emotional, and mental connection existed, too.

But at the time, I didn't really care. All I was concerned about was the fact that a *hot girl was interested in me.*

Within a week of that first meeting, she and I began dating. We kissed on the second date. We got a little crazy on her elf-sized couch on the third date. For every three physical steps we took, the guilt that drenched our "frustrated" souls forced us to take a step or two back. We'd pray about it. Refocus our steps. And try again. But within a couple of days of those new promises, we'd almost always jump over the first three steps and then take a few more.

Eventually, *within a month's time*, we were looking sex in the face, yet we resisted the temptation to go that far. But flirting with the thought certainly became somewhat addictive. So nearly every time we got together, we'd "flirt" right up to the line.

Fourteen weeks after our first meeting at that praise-and-worship concert, our relationship ended on a complication. Of course, we did make a couple fleeting attempts to rekindle the flame. Sometimes it would be her experiencing a weak moment. Other times it would be me. It took us almost a year to fully let go.

Prior to our meeting, both Jennifer and I had made mistakes in other relationships. And those mistakes had left us very much broken. Of course, neither of us would have recognized ourselves as broken. I think we were both hoping that the other would fix our brokenness. And even though there was a heartfelt attempt from both of us to direct our relationship toward Christ, my brokenness was crippling my ability to think about anyone but myself. Healing—real healing—rarely happens when you're inside a relationship and looking to please yourself.

Thankfully, both of us eventually journeyed our own directions and each found our true loves. But before I could even begin to learn how to love and be intimate with a woman in a pure and holy manner, I had to first become intimate with Jesus.

When I think back on the mistakes I've made in relationships, every one was a result of my own selfishness, because I entered relationships hoping to get served, not to be the one who serves. Over the years, I've learned that the holy part of my life doesn't begin with my actions. It starts with the condition of my heart; it's my heart that gauges "how far" I'm willing to sacrifice my own needs for the needs of the person I love.

But no line exists. Well, unless you consider intercourse God's line [*which you probably don't, if you're really honest with yourself*] because that's the only line that's clearly stated verbatim in the Bible. I do know Christian couples who have felt pure getting as close to intercourse as they could get without doing it. And I've known those who have felt purity demanded them to stay far away from that line. Truly, what is sin for one Christian couple might be innocent passion for another.

But biblically, I cannot make a sin versus righteousness argument for either side. I have my own opinion, of course. But I've also made my own mistakes. However, what I do find in Scripture is much talk about God desiring our hearts to be pure.

Though it may not be a specific line, the condition of your heart will play out in every aspect of your relationship — the emotional, mental, spiritual, and physical. And I believe a healthy, God-honoring relationship looks to build on all four of these areas while a couple is dating, engaged, and throughout their marriage. All four are important. And God should be in each.

How do we pursue this in a godly manner? I believe we have to look to Jesus. Only Jesus will make purity within a relationship truly possible. He's the only one who can make our hearts pure.

Consider rereading the Beatitudes (Matthew 5:1-12).

Read these words every day if you must. Because in these short but potent words of Jesus, I believe we Christians will find—or rediscover—what we need to know about living life the way our Savior intended, our premarital and marital sexual lives included. Jesus' call for humility, purity, peacemaking, and truth are all reflected in our hearts' desire to truly abandon everything our flesh says is true and follow him. We can't do this alone; that's why God has given us his Spirit to help us make choices in our daily lives. Listen to the Spirit inside of you. It's the Spirit who will lead you in your path to know God's "line" for your life. But I must tell you, that line will be selfless; in other words, *it won't be about you.*

Let me be frank: It's hard to not think about your own will for the sake of another. Of course, this struggle can happen at any time throughout your life. My wife and I struggle with this often in every area of our lives. Only when we stop thinking about ourselves do we get to the other side where our gaze gets set back on what Jesus wants and desires for us.

Only a couple in which both people are striving for Jesus will realize that true joy, intimacy, and sexiness is found in loving each other selflessly—*not* in the answer to "how far is too far?"

If you're still looking for that answer, consider the possibility that you might be asking the *wrong* question, unless you're

Three Ideas For Pure Premarital Intimacy

1 Clean each other's bathroom. Ooh, baby. Why not sacrifice your pride to the one you love by getting down on your hands and knees and giving your loved one's bathroom the cleaning job of its life? Scrub the toilet. Wipe off the vanity. Disinfect the shower. You might *still* be sexually frustrated after doing this, but both of you will certainly be smiling.

2 Look through each other's wallet. Exchanging wallets can be totally hot and so revealing. Show him your driver's license picture. Let her hold your credit card. Run your fingers through each other's old receipts. You never know what you'll learn while frolicking through the private sectors of each other's wallet. I recommend taking it slow.

3 Feed each other seedless grapes. Toss them in. Eat them out of each other's hands. Serve them with whipped cream and a bottle of sparkling cider. Get alone on a beach or in a park and enjoy. Trust me, grapes are your friends.

asking it in reference to "how far is too far in serving, loving, and being passionate about the one you love?" Then the answer is easy: A "too far" line for being a servant doesn't exist.

Okay, this part is beginning to sound like Max Lucado wrote it. So before I lose myself completely, I should probably wrap this up. I'll talk a little more about all this in the final section.

But before you move on to section 4, here are a few "intimate" ideas you and your honey might find irresistibly titillating. [And your pastor won't complain one bit.]

Marriage and Sex

[what you need to know before —
so you can perform after — you say I do]

> What a happy and holy fashion it is that those who love one another should rest on the same pillow.
>
> — Nathaniel Hawthorne

News flash: Before you get married, you need to know a thing or two about sex. Did you get that? I'll say it like Dr. Phil just to be sure.

BEFORE YOU GET MARRIED, YOU NEED TO KNOW A THING OR TWO ABOUT SEX!!

Oh, don't laugh. You'd probably be surprised at how many Christians go into married sex the same way jocks choose a new restaurant. They don't look at the menu ahead of time. They ignore the waiter's recommendation to try the special. And because they're afraid to try anything new, they order a burger and fries.

If you want a burger-and-fries sex life, well, okay, I guess that's entirely up to you. But I have a feeling that's not the case. Wouldn't you rather have a steak?

Of course, thankfully, most of you have already called ahead and made reservations [you know, marriage]. Which is certainly a good start. A needed start.

However, simply having a reservation doesn't guarantee a fine-dining experience. Sure, you'll get fed. And you'll probably go home full. But wouldn't you like to be full of good food versus something that tastes like it could have been made at Shoney's? And here's the deal: The difference between exquisite dining and simply having dinner is more often than not found in the details.

Sex has a lot of detail.

So in an effort to prepare you for what you might expect, what you need to look out for, and what you should aim toward experiencing, I offer you a section that gives you a lot of information you need to know before you get naked with your husband or wife. Don't expect this section to prepare you for everything, but it will certainly give you a lot of "food" for thought.

Don't worry about me sharing too much of the dirty [but holy] details; TH1NK [my publisher] and their evil sex editors will be sure to keep this section at least PG-13. However,

Why Can't We Just Call It Sex?

[Funny ways Christians describe sex]

The perpetuation of genital union. ChristianityToday.com describes it like this. Sounds hot, huh?

One-flesh intimacy. Found this one at Family.org. Of course, I know what they're trying to say, but it still sounds a little strange. Try saying to your spouse, "Hey, baby, let's go have some one-flesh intimacy in the bedroom" with a straight face.

Marital obligation. Okay, I know what this means. I heard a sermon on sex once where the preacher refused to say "sex." He called it "marital obligation" throughout the sermon. After a while, it sounded more like a jail sentence than something meant to be fun.

I'm going to try to sneak in a couple R-rated moments. But the great thing about marriage and sex is that even the R-rated moments are G-rated in God's eyes.

You shouldn't be reading this section if . . .

. . . you're a nun.

. . . you're under the age of eighteen [unless you get your parents' permission before you do. *I don't want your parents calling me*].

. . . you're my mother.

Coming Soon to a Lifestyle Near You: CHANGE

"They say that the first time you have sex the experience changes you," said Heather Locklear in a television interview I was watching. "I think that's actually scientific," she continued. "I certainly believe it; the first time I had sex, I could have sworn my breasts got bigger." *[Laughs]*

As I sat listening to the interview, Heather's statement intrigued me. The mere thought that there might be evidence proving first-time sex changes a person certainly interested me.

One time before, I had heard something similar. An old high school buddy had told me that sex put hair on a man's chest. He told us in the locker room once that his excess chest follicles happened because he lost his virginity when he was fourteen. At the time, I figured he was lying because he was insecure about being the hairiest teenage boy any of us had ever seen.

When Heather's interview went to a commercial break, I looked at my friend, who was watching the interview with me, and asked, "Do you think that's true? Do you think sex changes people?"

My friend looked at me strangely. "MATTHEW, please tell me you're not taking her statement seriously," he said.

I hesitated. I had actually begun thinking about whether or not I would experience physical change after sex.

"Of course I'm not," I said as convincingly as possible. "But the concept that a first-time sexual experience might bring change to a person's life is certainly interesting, don't you think?"

"OH MY GOSH! We're watching an interview with Heather Locklear, Matthew!" he said in a loud, tone-drenched voice. "HEATH-ER LOCK-LEAR! She's a bad TV actress. And you're taking her seriously! That worries me!" [My friend hated Heather Locklear.] "All I'm saying, Matthew, is that you better fact-check that information before you go around quoting it. There probably isn't any study. Think about what she said: '*They* say that the first time you have sex, it changes you.' Did she tell us who said this? Did she offer any evidence to support the statement? No! That's my point."

The next day, I tried Googling Heather's "scientific" information. And from what I could tell, there was no such evidence to support her theory. It seemed my friend was correct.

[Just in case Oprah chooses my book for her book club, I don't want her accusing me of lying. She has the power to rip anybody's life into a million little pieces.]

[Two months later]

The morning after our wedding night, my wife and I had to wake up early so we could attend a gift-opening party with all of our closest friends and family. As you can probably imagine, a gift-opening party was exactly what I wanted to do the day after my wedding night. [Insert the appropriate amount of sarcasm here. 📅]

However, much to my frustration, when ten o'clock rolled around, my wife and I were hobnobbing with sixty people who knew exactly what we'd been doing the night before. And they could certainly tell what we had been doing. We went to that party looking like two people who had just experienced sexual intercourse for the first time.

Tired eyes? ✔
Pale faces? ✔
Subtle grins? ✔

Fifteen minutes after our grand entrance, one of my sisters leaned over the table where a group had gathered and whispered, "So how was it?"

"How was *what*?" I asked sarcastically.

"You know what I'm talking about," she said.

I laughed. "Unbelievable," I whispered, not wanting to make it obvious to my mother, my younger sister, my pastor, my pastor's wife, and several other older, conservative-acting Christians I had known for a long time that I was talking about my first romp in the sack. I've always been an open person, but it wasn't like I wanted to advertise. Besides, I hadn't planned a speech.

My younger sister Elisabeth leaned into the conversation. "What are you two laughing about?" she asked.

Kelley whispered into Elisabeth's ear the gist of our conversation.

"You were able to actually do it? On my wedding night, sex hurt. We didn't get it done once."

The three of us laughed.

My mother, looking over at us laughing, exclaimed confidently, "I know exactly what you three are talking about." Elisabeth leaned over and whispered into my mother's ear.

My mother's eyes widened. "Well, I don't want to hear about it."

"I kinda do," shouted Elisabeth.

"Preacher," said my mother, looking over at the man who had proclaimed Jessica and me husband and wife, "you might want to go somewhere else, because knowing my son and how open he can be, he's apt to share every little detail about last night."

"Oh, I know, Carole," he said. "Why do you think I'm hanging around?"

Everyone erupted into laughter.

For forty minutes, we sat around the table and talked about sex. In fact, we talked openly about sex until one of my single groomsmen came around. When he sat down, the sex chatter stopped. It was like everyone knew a secret code to refrain from talking further. Apparently, a single twenty-four-year old Christian man is too innocent and fragile to hear married people talk positively and humorously about sex.

Then it dawned on me that only fourteen hours earlier I may have been deemed too immature for this conversation, too. I couldn't help but sit there and think that perhaps Heather Locklear had been right after all; sex brings change.

For some of you, it will be a drastic change. For others, you'll hardly recognize it. The amount of change you experience greatly depends on your sexual history. But here are a few things many Christians experience post-sex [within marriage].

1. You realize it's okay to talk about sex.

Okay, so you're not going to want to go into graphic detail, but you can certainly talk about it. I recommend in certain situations [especially at church], you should use "code." A fellow Sunday school teacher once told me that he needed to get home right after church so the ole pork tenderloin could get a good marinating. I knew exactly what he was talking about.

2. A good majority of Christians still aren't willing to listen.

So this somewhat contradicts what I just wrote in the paragraph above this one, but I feel like I should give you the full picture. Some married Christians think sex is a very private conversation. But don't let this scare you; you'll eventually know who and who not to talk sex to.

3. You may experience post-traumatic purity disorder.

For the first month or two after marriage, many Christians will experience what I like to call "post-traumatic purity disorder." Usually it occurs when you wake up in the morning and realize you're naked and lying next to your naked spouse. In a sudden lapse of thinking, you panic: "Oh my gosh, I AM SINNING! What have I done?" Usually a few seconds later, after your heart is beating fast and your mind is racing in a thousand different directions, you remember, "Oh, I'm married; this isn't a sin. God's happy for me." If P.T.P.D. events occur six to eight weeks into your marriage, you need help. Okay?

4. Church people treat you more adult-like.

As ridiculous as this might seem, whether you're single at twenty-three or thirty-three, there's always a few church people who don't treat you like a "grown up." Getting married and having sex seems to be the final step in maturity to some Christians. So anticipate some of your church peeps treating you like you've finally finished puberty.

5. You experience a pretty harsh bout with constipation.

Yes, constipation. Because you're not used to sharing a bed with another human being [or at least not without feeling a lot of guilt], you spend the first couple of weeks not wanting to fart in front of each other [at least, not when you're naked in bed]. Sometimes this can cause things to get a little backed up. Especially since most of you don't have separate bathrooms. And you're afraid to *really go* around your lover. [This point cannot be scientifically proven.]

Sex and Marriage, Sex and Marriage/Go Together Like a Horse and Carriage

[and ride that carriage often]

When I spoke to Christian "sexpert" Linda Dillow about the importance of sexual intimacy, she said, "Matthew, sex isn't supposed to be the most important thing in a marriage, but when it's not there or it's somehow not equally enjoyed by both partners, it *becomes* the most important thing." Linda's right—extremely right. I'm not sure she could be more right in her thinking.

Okay, so I'll break it down just in case you were indeed born yesterday: Sex is a highly important facet of marriage, like super important. You remember what the Bible says about sex, right? [Hint: I wrote about it in section 2.]

In marriage, like in the rest of your life, holy and healthy sexual living is the expectation. But within marriage, h & h living is about pursuing sexual freedom, sexual understanding, and sexual synergy with your spouse.

Your ability to pursue sexual freedom with no restraint inside the boundaries of your marriage is extremely important to its well-being. A healthy and holy sexual lifestyle brings a great deal of strength, depth, and stability to a marriage relationship that, like Linda's statement implied, when absent can affect a couple's spiritual, emotional, and physical core.

Sex is about more than just nudity and orgasms. Sure, those things ARE important and of course are two of the best parts of sex. But you might be shocked to learn how many components of your life and your personal happiness are affected by the sex life of you and your spouse. Of course, you won't be shocked for long because I have provided a nice sidebar for you to read (see next page) that details a few personal areas that sex affects.

Remember this: Sex is not the be-all and end-all, but when it's not there, it can greatly affect certain areas of your personal psyche and can eventually affect your marriage.

Married Sex Is a Journey

I'm getting ready to assume something about you and your knowledge about sex. Sure, your wisdom of all things sex might be a bit limited, but I'm going to take for granted that you know the events that have to happen to constitute "intercourse." Am I wrong in assuming you already know that sexual *intercourse* is when the penis [guy] gets inserted into the vagina

The married spark. The spark is the "aha" moment you experienced when you realized you were standing in front of the person you would one day marry. *That's the spark.* As you might assume, sex can help you keep that spark ALIVE! [Insert televangelist voice here. 😊] Sex can be an integral part of growing your marriage when it's boring or uninspiring. Pursuing the best that sex has to offer can help intensify the marriage spark into the passionate flame you desire. [Now, that sounded like Dr. Phil.]

Ego of an individual. All of us have egos. Yes, women have egos, too. And I promise you this: A holy and healthy sex life does wonderful things for our egos. Sex can bring good or bad feelings to a person's existence. Sure, sex is meant to bring physical pleasure, but the personal "return on investment" is often more important than the orgasm. I know, what could possibly be better [and more important] than the orgasm? However, a hot sex life helps both the man and woman feel needed, desired, and sexy. *And that's SO important.* The "ego" might be different depending on your personality, but no matter if you're male or female, you need your spouse to look at you and be overwhelmed with desire for you, your body, your pleasure, and your complete fulfillment. Good sex helps make that happen. [Of course, let me say this: *Good sex doesn't just happen.* So don't expect the beginning of your marriage to be filled with orgasmic heights. Especially if you're a woman. However, that doesn't mean you can't work toward it . . . and work hard.]

Mental stability. So not having a Solomonesque marriage — you know, one that comes complete with lush, vine-ripened grapes and leaping gazelles — will not guarantee depression or OCD. You're not likely to end up at the funny farm over bad or unengaged married sex. But sex does affect how you think about your marriage. A person with the sexual prowess of this ancient king [but inside only one marriage] is likely to have good thoughts about marriage. Good sex — because it ignites confidence, security, and the feeling of a 'job well done' — will no doubt help you think positively about the state of your relationship. It certainly shouldn't define it, but it will stimulate your brain [and a few other parts of your body] to visualize your marriage as close, passionate, and hope-filled. A couple with a good sex life isn't guaranteed to think perfectly about their relationship, but no doubt it's a part of the foundation that leads a husband and wife toward good, healthy mental stability about their marriage.

Emotional constancy. You don't want to cry like Paula Abdul on a special edition of *48 Hours,* do you? Of course not. Nobody wants his or her emotions to be the reason a network's ratings fly through the roof. Well, then, pursue married sex like a lion goes

[girl]? Hopefully, your sexual history includes the learning of this knowledge. If not, then call me. We can cry together.

No doubt the event that I just described is an amazing thing.

Yes, sex is amazing. Sex is so amazing that it might be the only thing powerful enough to make even the most devout atheist sing the "Hallelujah Chorus" once in a while — though maybe not at the beginning of marriage. Of course, I've never witnessed an atheist singing Handel's *Messiah*, but if I did, I think it would be pretty cool. However, like I mentioned in section 2, as amazing as sex is, it's also just a little weird. Okay, so maybe it's a lot weird. Only God could have thought up the idea that a man would stick a thing called a penis [a rather weak name for

after her prey. Maybe not exactly like a lion, but you know what I mean. Sexuality within a marriage relationship is highly emotional — affection, masculinity, femininity, compassion, safety, to name a few. Your emotions are tied more to your sexuality than you know. We don't necessarily know how we will react emotionally to married sex. What you do — and do not do — in the bedroom can influence the emotional outlook of you and your spouse.

Spiritual congruency. God wants you to have hot sex with your spouse. Here's a more Christian explanation: God holds dear the sexual relationship between a husband and wife. In other words, he desires you to have an UNBELIEVABLE sexual lifestyle. When you and your spouse are pleasing each other sexually, you will also be fulfilling God's spiritual design for your marriage. Sex is supposed to make couples closer, more in tune with each other's needs. Okay, enough with the schmaltz; here's the deal: When sex is happening in your marriage, and happening well and often and *loudly*, God is pleased.

✳ ✳ ✳

Because each couple is made up of two unique individuals, the facets of marriage that sex affects will vary. Before a couple marries, they should talk to each other about how each of them views sex. It's important to have some kind of idea about your future mate's sexual expectations.

such a miraculous object] into a woman's vagina [an even weirder name for an even more miraculous object]. In that section, I wrote about God having to tell Adam and Eve how it was done. I wonder what God thought as he watched Adam and Eve do it for the first time. Was he tempted to stop and say, "No, no, no, Adam! That's NOT how it's done! I create something wonderful and you have to go and mess it up. Sorry, Eve; he'll get this right eventually."

Being the Supreme Being that he is and one known for his frequent disappointment in the performances of humanity, it's not that big of a stretch to assume he might have thought about giving them some pointers.

I have a confession to make: Over the years, I have found much intrigue thinking and talking about this very topic — you know, [whispering this] Adam and Eve's sex life.

>>Perhaps I should add some context to this confession. Is it strange that I've spent a great deal of time contemplating the sexual lifestyle of Adam and Eve? Am I in the minority on this one? It's okay; I can handle the truth.

You already know that I grew up in a strict church. Most of the time, sexuality was stifled and presented negatively inside the walls of my church. Because of that, biblical literature became the only outlet where I felt comfortable and guiltless engaging my leashed-up curiosity. Consequently, I found the sexual tension of Adam and Eve's love story to be, at times, powerfully arousing. Let me explain.

My freshman art history professor walked into the college classroom one morning bickering about religion. This time he was verbalizing his frantic dislike for a group of Christians who were protesting a nationally known museum's display of an art exhibit, one that displayed well-known biblical stories by using strong sexualized overtones. The group won. "This is why I hate religion!" said my professor. "It keeps good people from thinking for themselves. And it keeps us from getting to see good art. I just hate it."

The older professor stopped talking and walked over to a large case that was filled with copies of what he considered great art. He rummaged through the paintings for a few moments, looking for the one that would make this morning's antireligion lecture relevant to the class.

"Here it is," he purred, pulling out a large poster-sized print of painter Lucas the Elder Cranach's work *Adam and Eve*. "Look at this painting. Religion might make some angry, just like it does me, but without it, the world would never have experienced some of the sexiest art I have ever witnessed." Professor Blackwell smiled sarcastically. "Thanks be to God for this wonderful gift."

The class laughed.

The painting was indeed sexy and led me on an exploration of sorts to discover the true nature of Adam and Eve's sex life. So basically I just began asking other Christians their thoughts on the topic. **And thus, the context of my intrigue over the first man and the first woman.** <<

What You Didn't Learn from Your Parents About Sex Presents:
Answers to Your Most Intriguing Sex Questions!

QUESTION: Dear editors, I'm getting married in a couple of months, and I have a problem. I'm nervous that my future wife won't be satisfied with my "size." So here's my dilemma: Does size matter to Christian women? — Jeff, 23, graduate student

ANSWER: Hello, Jeffrey! We hate that so many guys feel such insecurity about the size of their penis. And in today's culture, the supposed "remedies" are everywhere; advertisers never cease to remind men that "bigger is *always* better." But we're not convinced. So don't waste your time and money on pills and pumps. However, let's be honest; hearing from us that size does not matter is probably not going to help you feel better about your situation. You've heard all this information before, right? Well, we decided to ask a

But anyway, it's been my experience, when talking to people about Adam and Eve's sexual performance, that most Christians think their sex life was close to *perfect*. They imagine Adam being a well-endowed man with muscles and a six-pack. They think of Eve having large breasts, a flat stomach, and legs a mile and a half long. [I admit that most of the people I have talked to about this have been guys, but not all.] Most think the first couples' sexual skill would make today's porn stars seem, well, about as sexy as dog dung in the middle of a living room floor. [Good analogy, huh?]

Honestly, I like thinking that this is true. I believe God-followers should be having the best sex. I think we should be setting the standard on sexuality. I think those who fear God should have so much sexual freedom within their marriage that non-Christians would look at us and become overwhelmingly jealous. Of course, we will never know what Adam and Eve's sex life was like. But one thing is for sure: If their sexual lifestyle was the kind that would put to shame the porn stars of today, they probably didn't get that way on the first try. Nor the second. Nor the third. They would have had to realize that their sexual lifestyle — the pursuit of pleasure, intimacy, and orgasmic heights — was indeed a journey, one that required two people to dedicate themselves to a lifetime together.

When you get married, you begin the journey, too. When it comes to sex, that might be the most important thing to know:

bunch of young Christian women what they thought. Here are some of their responses:

I don't think penis size is important. There are far more important things to think about. — Janna, 22

Well, being that I am a virgin and plan on being one when I get married, I think whatever my man is packin' will be fine with me. — Sierra, 19

Guys make such a HUGE deal over the size of their penises. *Give me a break!* I want my husband to be secure in his manhood. There is nothing more unattractive than a guy who is not secure. — Hope, 25

See, Jeff? Women aren't too concerned about size; they're more interested in how guys *bring it*. We're pretty sure your wife will love you for who you are, but the question is this: Will *you* love you for who you are?

Tootles! We think you're sweet!

>>The editors

PS: Send us an e-mail at WeLoveWritingForMatthew@ yahoo.com.

Sex is a journey. So many make it a destination. So many make it something that becomes boring or unfulfilling. So many make it just an add-on, a bonus, a marital duty.

If you desire a sexually successful marriage [and really, who doesn't desire that?], you and your spouse must dedicate [and rededicate and rededicate] yourselves to the sexual journey of marriage.

Don't feel weird about how God made our bodies to respond to sex. Learn about it. It's an unbelievable thing that God created our bodies fully capable of such happenings. People who view their married sexual lifestyle as a journey will continue to educate themselves about sex throughout their marriages.

The Basics [About Sex] You Need to Know

You know that the penis gets inserted into the vagina. That's a pretty good start. For those of you who didn't know that [well, at least until reading it a few pages back], you might be feeling a little peculiar right about now.

But for most of us, the penis/vagina knowledge is something we have known since middle school. At least, we pretended to know in middle school. Once a fellow classmate — she was a tenth grader; I was in eighth grade — asked me if I knew how to have sex. I said, "Oh my, yes. You don't have to worry about me; I'd know what to do." That was a lie. I thought a woman had a fajita, remember?

In eighth grade, my lack of knowledge about women was *sad*, but it didn't hurt anything. However, when you're preparing to get married, what you don't know can affect your married life. But hopefully if the evil sex editors at TH1NK don't edit everything I write, you'll be a bit more informed by the time you finish reading this section.

What Women Should Know About Men
[As It Relates to Sex]

Ladies, this part of the book is for you. Guys, you're welcome to read along, but I don't think you're going to learn anything new here. So, ladies, here are a few things you should know about your man. This is certainly not everything [as I'll confess a lot in this book], but it will get you started.

Let's begin with the penis.

The penis is a funny topic. For some of you, just reading the word [I'll whisper it: *penis*] is making you feel a little awkward. This is more common than you might imagine. It's not a pandemic. But apparently, quite a few Christian women suffer from a disorder called the "I'm afraid of the word *penis*" syndrome. I know this disorder exists because I had a friend who had the condition.

Her name is Christina. And according to her, "Good Christian girls can usually get away without ever using the word *penis*, at least until they have babies." Of course, being the type of person who likes to understand people's reasoning, I decided to ask her about her fear.

"Why don't you like the word *penis*?" I asked her one afternoon.

"It's such a gross word, Matthew," Christina shrieked in her Southern accent. "And I don't *ever* need to say it. I affectionately describe it as a tallywacker or peepee."

"A *WHAT*?!? It's not called a *tallywacker*!" I retaliated. "It's a penis."

"I don't care what you call it; I'm calling it what I want to," she said stubbornly.

"Okay. But I can assure you that your husband is never going to want you to refer to his sexual member as a tallywacker or peepee. You're almost thirty, Christina. I think you're old enough to use the proper terminology."

"You might be right. But you know, Matthew, it's hard to break away from what my momma taught me. And she hated the word *penis*; my husband will just have to get over it."

Christina's future husband hopefully will be able to get over it. It doesn't seem like that big of a deal to you, huh? Well, ladies, that's because you don't have one. If you did, you'd understand.

Do You Know Your Man?

[a quiz about the male genitalia]

If you pass this quiz, you can consider yourself informed about your husband's penis. If you get more than two wrong, then you need to read about the penis at TheMarriageBed.com.

1. What is the name for the sack-like object that is located behind the penis? _____

2. What is the most sensitive area of the penis? _____

3. In what part of the male genitalia is sperm produced?
_____

4. What is an erection?
_____

5. If a man has been circumcised, what does that mean?
_____

6. What do you call the whitish fluid that is emitted from the penis during ejaculation?
_____

7. True or false: A man's shoe size is directly related to the size of his penis. _____

8. Name the two places from which 99 percent of semen comes: _____ and
_____

ANSWERS: 1. Scrotum **2.** The glans. Also referred to as the head **3.** The testicles **4.** When the penis hardens due to its spongelike tissue being filled with blood **5.** The foreskin of his penis has been removed **6.** Semen **7.** False **8.** The prostate and seminal vesicles

The penis is his friend [and he wants it to be yours, too]. Ladies, what you may or may not know about guys is this: Most of us have a strange connection with our penis. We're not sure why, really, but for a majority of guys, it's a phenomenon we've experienced for a while. This emotional and physical connection has been a part of our lives since we first discovered our manhood at age four. We think of our penis as a friend or an alter ego. Some of us have even named it and refer to him using the name. We have no idea if this thing we feel is God-given, like an instinct we're born with, or if it's learned behavior. But let me be frank. Your husband, if he's shy, a private person, or unable to express himself, probably won't admit this, but a part of him has been looking forward to introducing you to his penis. He's hoping that you will grow to like it as much as he likes it. In fact, he's hoping the two of you will be BFF [best friends forever]. I know this is difficult for you to understand; a lot of us guys don't get it either. But please, for your husband's sake, play along. It won't kill you to love your husband's friend, will it? Oh, and one more thing: Go ahead and assume this about your husband until he tells you otherwise. Don't *ever* offend his penis. Anything that might offend his penis will more than likely offend him. Basically, if you treat his penis with half the love you feel for chocolate, you're on the right track. Hey, try mixing the two. It might help things along.

In other words, if you want your husband to know you find him incredibly attractive, if you want to boost his masculinity, and if you want him to be happy, learn to love his penis. This is certainly not the only way, but it's an important one.

Men actually do need sex — some think men can't help it.

What can I say? Sex is a curse guys must live with, I suppose. However, most guys are willing to live with it. Here's the deal: According to TheMarriageBed.com, a website dedicated to helping Christian married couples pursue satisfying sexual lifestyles, a man actually has a need for sexual release on a regular basis. It's not our fault; it's our bodies' fault. You see, men have these glands called seminal vesicles. Inside these two small glands, the majority of fluid that makes up semen is produced. As semen is produced, the glands fill up [much like a bladder] and eventually need to be released. According to the peeps at TheMarriageBed.com, these glands fill up every twenty-four to seventy-two hours. So, yeah, I'm saying this: Guys *need* sex. I know; you're not buying it, huh? Hey, look it up yourself.

Sometimes he wants you to pursue him.

Guys don't mind pursuing you for sex. However, most men like it when their wives take the initiative once in a while and pursue them for some lovemaking. Guys love it when their wives take control of a situation. Of course, make sure he's in the right mind-set for your "taking charge." Your husband might not want to be sexually assaulted. Then again, some guys like it just fine. It all depends on your husband's personality type. As you get to know him sexually, you'll be able to read what kinds of moods best suit your getting behind the wheel and driving the car. Most important, when you're in the mood to take charge, don't mimic what you see on TV or in the movies. Be yourself. Be willing to laugh if something funny happens. Don't take stuff overly seriously; it's about pleasure, so have fun getting your man in the mood.

Ways to Pursue

He may never ask for it, but he'd love to see you . . .

◉ **Do a strip tease.** Flirt with him by putting on a little show. It doesn't have to be a Broadway number, just a three-minute dance to Usher will do. And you get bonus points if the underwear is hot.

◉ **Walk around naked.** Guys love seeing their wives naked. And not only in the bedroom. Most husbands want their wives to be secure in their skin. So don't be afraid to flaunt what you've got. Your man's spirit will soar seeing you be free once in a while. So surprise him.

◉ **Wake him up.** You know what I'm saying, right? Morning sex is hot. [Just brush your teeth first.]

◉ **Let him lie back and just enjoy.** Once in a while, give your husband a break on "performing." Tell him that you want him doing nothing except concentrating on himself.

We can't help this; it's how most of us were made.

While God designed women to experience multiple orgasms in one session, he programmed men differently. In the past, I have envied the ability to experience an orgasm again and again and again. But I've come to the conclusion that God really did know what he was doing. Can you imagine a world where men were easily able to achieve multiple orgasms? You think the world has problems now? It wouldn't compare to what might occur if God hadn't equipped us with the need to "recover" after an orgasm.

The problem happens when we do it too quickly. Early on in marriages, a man's sexual stamina might be lacking. And you might suffer [well, not really suffer, just not get pleasured] because of this. But with a little bit of time and a lot of practice, we get better.

Just thought you should be aware of the possible quick trigger. Oh, and sometimes when we get old, the whole quick trigger thing could happen again. That's all I'm going to say about that.

Sex and a man's life.

For most men [again, not all], sexuality is connected to other aspects of life. Like I wrote earlier in this section, a guy's sex life, whether it is good, bad, holy, or lust-filled, can impact him emotionally, mentally, *and* spiritually. I'm certainly not suggesting that it's your responsibility to make sure your husband is sexually pure; it's not. But in knowing how a man is wired, it will certainly help you understand his needs, his desires, and how the sexual relationship the two of you create together plays out in his everyday life.

For a guy, sex is about more than just a quick wham-bam. A good, spirited sexual lifestyle within marriage is also a source of mental and emotional stability for a guy. Though sex doesn't complete him, it's more than likely true that a man works better when his married sex life is good. He loves better when it's good. His ego is fed [and that's not a bad thing]. He's more passionate in certain areas of his life. He feels alive.

Five Statements Men and Women Should Feel the Freedom to Say

One of the most important aspects of a holy and healthy sexual lifestyle is your ability to communicate your feelings openly, honestly, and without fear. As you'll read throughout this section, communication is important to a good married sex life. Here are five statements you should always feel comfortable saying:

- "This makes me feel uncomfortable."
- "Hey, can we try . . . ?"
- "How can I make this experience better for you?"
- "You know, if you did *this*, it would drive me wild."

However, it's not just about getting some. It's also about how a wife views her husband sexually outside of the bedroom. Does she build up that side of his character? Do her words and encouragement make him feel sexy?

When my wife looks at me and tells me she thinks I'm the sexiest man alive [and she does it quite often], it does something to me. Sure, I know that I'm not the sexiest man alive, but knowing that my wife thinks so makes my spirit soar. Before dating and marrying Jessica, I didn't know that a woman's willingness and freedom to express her sexual attraction for me would benefit me like it does. But it's a huge boost in my life. It's by no means the center of my life or my marriage, but her words do touch every aspect of who I am.

 Fact: Some Guys Find Intimacy in More Than Just Sex

Some professionals claim that men find their intimacy right before and during sex. Well, if this were true, that would imply that before getting married, every man trying to stay pure would never have experienced intimacy. But I don't think this is true. Sure, guys like sex a lot. But some men actually do find intimacy through situations, events, and affection other than getting their sexual groove on. And if they don't, it might mean they need to learn how.

Four Things a Guy Needs From His Wife

1 **Affirmation.** Make him feel like he's one in a million. Once in a while when he's naked, tell him it's taking every ounce of your energy not to jump his bones.

2 **Security.** Show your husband how much you love having sex with him. Send him an e-mail telling him "how great last night was." Sure, this sounds simple, but your words and actions will leave him feeling confident in your relationship.

3 **Your desire.** Sex for a man is about getting it on. But it's also about whether or not he thinks you're enjoying it. When he knows that you're fully engaged in the sexual process, it only makes him feel that much more secure and confident in his marriage.

4 **Communication.** Men often tend to see only what's directly in front of them. They need to be told how their actions are making you feel [the good and the bad].

Well, ladies, you are now moderately informed about men and sex. Oh, there's a TON more I could have covered, but this is enough to get you on the right track. Before you get married, you might consider reading *Intimate Issues* by Linda Dillow and Lorraine Pintus and *Intimacy Ignited* by Linda, Lorraine, and their husbands, Joseph and Peter. And if you are already married, you still might consider reading these books.

What Men Need to Know About Women
[As It Relates to Sex]

Christians say a lot of things about the sexuality of women. Much of what is said is built on stereotypes that I'm not convinced are accurate for today's woman.

Every Young Man's Battle, a very passionate book that has awakened thousands of young men to the power of lust and the hold it can have on an individual, has this to say when attempting to give young men a "realistic" picture of women and marriage: "Women find their intimacy through things like touching, sharing, hugging, and communicating deeply."

As I read those words, I couldn't help but wonder if this was actually a true statement. Do women really get their primary intimacy from sharing and hugging? My wife balked at the implications of this statement. Of course, I value my wife's opinion. However, on top of that reasoning, a part of me questioned the statement because the book also stated that men pretty much find intimacy only before and during sexual intercourse. Although much of the book was interesting and helpful, I didn't agree with that statement. I'll admit that guys are sometimes a little shallow, but come on; I know lots of guys who enjoy forms of intimacy other than ones that result in orgasm.

But just because my wife and I disagree with the book's "touching, sharing, hugging, communicating" theory for women, I didn't want to base my thoughts in this book just on our assumptions. So I asked a few of my twentysomething female friends to tell me if this was indeed true.

The answers didn't surprise me, really.

"Are you kidding?" said one twenty-six-year-old married woman. "I think that's pretty limiting. Sure, I like to cuddle more than my husband does. But it doesn't replace my desire and need for sex."

Another woman, a twenty-nine-year-old teacher, had this to say: "That makes me laugh. I think it's sad that some Christians limit a Christian woman's intimacy to hugging and talking. Sure, I like that. But it's certainly not what I like the most."

However, while some books make women seem uninterested in sex, other books within the Christian publishing world unintentionally [I hope] make incorrect statements about women and sex.

In one popular Christian book we learn that women can be sexually satisfied without orgasm. Well, that's up for debate. While some women might be okay without the "heights" of pleasure for a short time, I'm not so sure every woman would agree with this claim. Although I should have known something was a bit peculiar with this book when the authors also make the claim that I'm able to reuse a condom. Yes, you read correctly. They even give instructions on how to clean it. *That's frightening to me.*

The young women who replied to my survey were looking forward to sex. They couldn't wait to experience love and passion and nakedness with their husbands in marriage. I wanted to know if those I interviewed were complete freaks. I even thought that perhaps my wife is a freak.

Because I am a guy, and not a professional sex therapist, I thought it might be good to hear a woman's perspective on this topic. So I asked my friend Kerri Pomarolli, author of the book *If I'm Waiting on God, Then What Am I Doing in a Christian Chatroom?*, to expound on what she believes women are looking for in the bedroom.

Kerri's Ramblings About Married Sex

So Matthew asked me to write about the Christian woman's perspective of sex. Of course, he wanted only a thousand words; I could seriously write thirty thousand words if given the chance. I mean, hello? I've been married for just a little over nine months; I think I totally qualify as an expert now that it's legal for me to be in bed with someone other than my Winnie-the-Pooh. [Hey, don't judge me.]

Here's the deal: When you get engaged, people suddenly begin throwing books about sex at you. I think this is hilarious. These books have some of the world's best titles. I suppose the authors of these books truly believe that while you're in bed with your honey, you'll also be reading your copy of *Sheet Music*, saying, "No, honey, diagram 1 says to raise your right arm — no, your right arm! Hey, I think we almost got it."

Actually, since I'm a type A woman, telling my husband what the book says to do might be right up my alley. I love giving directions.

Speaking of directions, I have something to say to the women. Ladies, do yourself a favor. Before you get married, make sure you tell yourself that you're actually going to speak up when you're in bed with your man. *Yes, speak up.* Hey, we talk when we're in the car, in the house, in the changing rooms at the Gap — heck, God-fearing women pretty much will talk anywhere given the chance. But for some reason, when we get in the bedroom, we stop talking. *Why is that?*

Since when are we women shy about asking for what we want? But in bed, we are. For whatever reason, when it comes to the sexual relationship with our husbands, a lot of us feel as though if we were to say anything, give instruction of any kind, or tell him exactly what we want, we might hurt our husband's feelings. And of course, we don't want to slow down his "mojo" — if you know what I mean.

But, ladies, come on; we're too nice in bed. I'd venture to say you'd rock your husband's world if you gave him a little positive affirmation when he does something that pleases you. Be a cheerleader when he's performing like a football star, but don't be afraid to offer some coaching tips here and there. Women, last time I checked, they can't read our minds, and I've yet to find any book for them that explains *thoroughly* how our complicated female machinery works. But you own the manual, so why not share it with the man who's going to be operating the car for the next fifty years? And to do that, you might have to open your mouth and talk.

Now, men, let me just speak to you for a moment. Because your involvement might really help the process here. Here's a secret: Your wife [or future wife] likes sex. *Yes, she likes it.* She doesn't see it as an obligation. I know you've heard that she sees it as an obligation, but it's more than likely *not* true. She might not always act like she likes sex — perhaps due to some past baggage or something — but trust me, she does. But if she's having trouble letting that *love* out, you have the power to help her feel comfortable enough in the bedroom to express herself sexually and, umm, make your sex life a little more fulfilling, too.

Guys, you need to ask her point-blank [repeat after me], "Honey, is there anything specific you'd like to tell me about our sex life that I could improve on?" Okay, say it again. Trust me, this is one of the biggest things a man can do to please his wife — let her feel free to communicate her feelings about sex. Ask her about what she likes and what she dislikes. You can even do this during the intimate moments. *No, really, you can.* We women love to talk. Sure, she might be shy at first, but you two are in this for the long haul. So why not work toward being open with each other now — even in the bedroom?

One more thing. Matthew is right to say that men too often think of sex as a destination. Women don't want to feel pressure. We don't want to feel rushed or pushed into anything. We may need some extra time to warm up to you sometimes. And again, sometimes we feel as though if we were to say that out loud, we may hurt your feelings. It's nothing personal, but sometimes we just need to have some time to clear our heads of whatever crisis we were just dealing with. *You know us; it could be any number of serious issues.*

Here's the deal: A woman's engine sometimes takes twice as long to turn on as a man's. But, boys, come on now; don't we all agree it's well worth the investment? Reassure your wife that you're not in a hurry. The best thing my husband could ever say to me is, "Whatever happens, happens . . ." and actually mean it.

Basically we women don't want to feel like we're playing beat the clock with our sex lives so you don't miss that last episode of *24*.

Five Things Kerri Said That are Worth Repeating

1. Ladies, don't be afraid to speak your mind.
2. Women do indeed like sex.
3. Guys, you have the power to help your wife open up to sexuality.
4. Guys, ask your wife questions about what she needs in the bedroom.
5. Don't miss the last episode of *24*.

Men: the proper treatment of wives.

Foreplay is of utmost importance. Yes, I know you can go from zero to sixty faster than a BMW 550i, but your wife most likely isn't wired that way. It might take her a little more time to work up to your speed. The best thing you can do is to think of foreplay as a round-the-clock occurrence. In other words, if you're looking to have sex at nine o'clock, help her with the dishes at five thirty, watch *American Idol* with her at seven, and then offer to give her a back massage at eight. My guess is that nine o'clock might come around thirty minutes early.

Make out with her. Remember what it felt like when you guys had just begun dating? All you were allowed to do was kiss and cop an innocent feel. Well, do it again as a married couple.

Touch her for no reason at all. Shock your wife by cuddling with her in front of the TV with no plans of getting some later. Women don't want to feel like objects. They want to be romanced, not manipulated.

Fantasy [to be continued]. You probably don't know this, but every time you make love to your wife, you're adding to the story she's writing in her head. While you see each sexual experience as an individual book [or perhaps a pamphlet], she sees each experience as a continuation of the last. Use your imagination and build on the story. Sometimes it might be as simple as lighting a few candles; other times it might be paying close attention to a particular spot on her body that you might often ignore.

Of course, there's so much more I could mention, but unfortunately, most of it is way too hot for this book. However, a few more hints are mentioned later on in this section.

A brief explanation of the vagina.*

As Kerri so eloquently put it, women have somewhat complicated machinery. And when you're used to only handling your own rather user-friendly equipment, the vagina can be a wee bit overwhelming. But if you're like most Christian men when they get married, you probably know one thing about the vagina *really* well: It's the place where the penis goes.

---

* This section was written with help from TheMarriageBed.com.

Well, it's a bit more than just that. Here are all the parts of the vagina that you should at least know by name and function.

The vulva. Okay, so the vulva — who named sexual organs? — is the outer and inner fleshy lips of the vagina. Some refer to it as the entire outer part [or visible part] of the vagina. As a woman becomes aroused, the vulva becomes engorged with blood, which causes it to swell and become deep red in color.

The clitoris. So, yeah, this part is important. In fact, when it comes to sex, a guy better know about the clitoris because it's the main area stimulated on a woman during sex. Some books describe it as the female equivalent to the penis. In fact, the clitoris has more nerve endings than the head of the penis. So when you get married, learn where this is, guys. Of course, you've seen the diagrams, right? Yeah, they don't help much. So don't be afraid to ask your wife to help you find it; her orgasmic pleasure depends on your finding it again and again and again [and again].

The opening of the vagina. Yes, this is where your penis will eventually go [when you're married, of course]. Most of the time, the vagina is only potential space because it's in an unaroused, collapsed state. During sexual arousal or foreplay, the vaginal tube wall [the outside layer known as the fibrous layer] creates a slippery fluid that serves as lubricant. This lubricant makes it easier for the penis to slip inside.

The hymen. The hymen is a fold of tissue that is located just inside the vagina. The editors explained this earlier in one of the questions. The hymen is the layer that you will break through [which may cause bleeding] when you insert your penis for the first time. However, like the editors said earlier, the hymen can be broken without intercourse by various activities. Because the hymen is quite elastic, breaking through it sometimes requires more than intercourse. If you and your wife are having trouble, see a gynecologist.

The G-spot. Okay, so this spot, located two to three inches inside the vagina on its roof, actually exists. [Yet, at times, I swear the spot moves. But I'm probably wrong.] It's named after Dr. Ernest Grafenberg, the first guy to duly note that this spot aided in erotic pleasures. Here's what TheMarriageBed. com says about the G-spot: "Some women are able to orgasm from G-spot stimulation alone, while others greatly enjoy the so-called blended orgasm resulting from a combination of clitoral and G-spot stimulation."

Guys, for a more thorough read about the vagina's magical parts, visit TheMarriageBed.com. You might learn something. Or you could keep flying blind; your choice.

Despite what you've heard or read before, the orgasm is important for women, too.

Can a woman enjoy sex without an orgasm? Yes. Will she enjoy it forever without an orgasm? Umm, probably not. However, at the beginning of marriage, it sometimes takes a couple a bit of time and experience before the wife reaches her sexual climax. Like I wrote earlier, sex is a journey. Mind-blowing experiences for your wife might not happen right away. And that's okay, as long as you're working to make the sexual experience more enjoyable for her. But here's the deal: All women are different. There's no "magic formula" I can give you that will guarantee the "hotness" level will reach the boiling point. Sometimes your wife will have too much on her mind to get there. Sometimes you might not be hitting the right spots. Sometimes it might be a physical condition that keeps her from experiencing an orgasm, and she might need to visit her doctor. And sometimes, you'll simply reach climax before she's ready to.

However, just because there isn't necessarily a magic formula doesn't mean you are powerless. Here's a game plan:

Go slowly. Yes, I say this a lot. But it's true. "Sexpert" Linda Dillow says a woman is like a Crock-Pot [slow] and a man is like a microwave oven [fast]. Regardless of how strange you think these comparisons are, they're still true. The longer you spend turning your wife on prior to intercourse, the better chance she will have to climax.

Practice stamina. When you first get married, you have an excuse to be a little quick on the draw. And that shouldn't embarrass you; it's normal. But over time, you should be practicing stamina. A little holding power can go a long way in making your wife sing [and shout] your praises.

Try different positions. This is extremely important. For one, some positions give you a little more staying power. But that's not all. As you try new things, your wife will discover positions that she enjoys.

Be patient. Resist the temptation to become frustrated with your wife. This might seem ridiculous now, but when you're in the heat of the moment, really wanting—and trying to help—your wife experience the joy of sex, frustration is completely possible. Most of the time, these kinds of situations are neither person's fault, just the nature of sex.

Mood Makers for Husbands

[pretend you totally knew these on your own]

Some guys are natural-born romancers. Some guys aren't. Both types might find an idea or two worth trying from the list below.

- ◙ Forty-five minutes, your hands, and massage lotion.
- ◙ Light candles and/or incense to create the ambiance for love.
- ◙ Pray with your wife. You might be surprised.
- ◙ Caramel sauce and your imagination.
- ◙ A long welcome-home kiss, with dinner already sitting on the table.
- ◙ Cuddle while watching a Reese Witherspoon movie [nope, *Walk the Line* doesn't count].
- ◙ Ask her to work out with you, then tell her the gym is in the bedroom.
- ◙ Send flirty e-mails to her Hotmail account; get her in the mood before she walks in the door.
- ◙ Do something spontaneous and sexy while sitting at a stoplight. Just don't hurt yourself.

What You Need to Know for a Magical Wedding Night

Forget the fact that everyone at your wedding wants you to stay at the reception. If you've been there for at least two hours, you have my permission to jet whenever you're ready. Believe me, your guests might look disappointed to see you two leaving the dance floor earlier than expected, but they'd do it in a heartbeat if it were their wedding day. So go ahead and leave whenever you darn well please. The wedding day is yours to spend how you see fit. And if you see fit to be naked with your honey by six thirty, when the reception began at five—*do it*. You don't have to explain why you want to get away. Believe me, everyone in the room knows exactly why you want to leave.

You will love your wedding night; it's the perfect mix of weird and amazing. So cherish it. I will certainly remember mine for the rest of my life. I won't remember it simply for its hotness, and it certainly had its hot moments. [Five hot moments, to be exact.] I will remember mine most for the mess we made of that hotel room; it wasn't just the tangled sheets but also the rose petals, spilled beverages, and bright purple feathers from something my wife wore. Wow. When we left the next morning, I peeked out the front door of the room to ensure that none of the cleaning people would see us leaving. I didn't want them being able to put faces to the mess we were leaving behind. I cannot imagine what those poor people must have talked about after our departure. Those who do hotel housekeeping must grow quite wearisome of honeymooners.

If you're wanting the perfect wedding night, you'd better read another book. However, if you want to know what to expect and how you can make your first time a good one, read on.

Wedding Night Time Line

Consider this time line a countdown to sex; this will give you some idea of what and when things need to get done.

One year prior: Get engaged. If your engagement is longer than fourteen months, consider moving it up. Do you really want to wait that long? *Didn't think so.*

Six to eight months prior: Begin thinking about hotel/bed-and-breakfast options. If your wedding is around a holiday, you might consider getting this reserved up to a year in advance. If you're able to, you might go to the hotel and handpick your room.

Six to eight months prior: Ladies, ask one of your friends to start planning a lingerie party. Sure, you don't want it to happen right now. But you want to give your friends plenty of warning. Your man will thank you [hopefully again and again].

Three months prior: Whichever one of you is in charge of making sure the hotel has all the necessary goodies [see shopping list on pages 232–233], begin thinking and planning for that now.

Two months prior: Double-check your hotel reservation. Just in case. This might also be a good time to find out what the room includes. Is there a CD player or iPod hookup? Does the room come with video capability? *Kidding.* Ask them if they're willing to hang a strobe light. Now, that's hot.

Three weeks prior: Go wedding-night shopping [get all the things on the list].

Three days prior: Guys, buy some new underwear. And no, I don't mean an $8.99 three-pack of boxer briefs. Go with something a little fancier. Heck, if you're kinky, you might try the special "trombone" briefs that are available. Let's just say these ditties make for quite the horn section, if you will. And you know what happens to horns, right? *Yeah.*

One day prior: If you're having fruit in the room, you might want to buy it or have someone from the wedding party do it.

Day of: Guys: trim, shave, or wax where necessary. Yes, *there*, too, if necessary.

Wedding night: Do it.

Shopping List

Most of these items are available at Target, Wal-Mart, or Walgreens. Of course, some of these items are optional, depending on the couple.

▧ **Personal lubricant.** You know, K-Y. However, K-Y is not most gynecologists' choice these days. Today most recommend Astroglide because it's less irritating to the female body. I sound like a commercial. If you're not sure what personal lubricant is for, you'll know soon enough.

▧ **Condoms.** Even if you're using another form of birth control, it's always a good idea to have condoms around just in case. [On our honeymoon, we lost our luggage for twenty-four hours, so just-in-case condoms became a necessity.] If you're not sure what brand to buy, go with the Durex Pleasure Pack. You get a variety. And variety is good.

▧ **Massage oil.** Don't go cheap on massage oil. Bath and Body Works has a wide selection of massage oils to choose from. If you're not sure about your future husband/wife's allergies, be sure to buy hypoallergenic and scent free. However, scents are nice.

▧ **Candles and matches.** Most hotel rooms do not provide candles because of fire hazards. So if you want a warm, glowing environment, make sure you bring your own.

▧ **Underwear.** Don't bring just any kind of underwear; bring something special and clean. When I say special, I mean sexy. When I say clean, I mean wait until you're in your honeymoon suite to put the "special underwear" on. If you've been dancing and/or nervously sweating, shower first. Hey, do it together if you're comfortable with that [but don't feel bad if you're not].

⊠   **"Extras."** Is chocolate syrup an option? Champagne? Rose petals? Handcuffs? Whatever fun "extras" you need, make sure you buy all of this ahead of time.

Other Things You Might Need

- ⊠ Toiletries
- ⊠ Change of clothes
- ⊠ Extra pair of underwear [maybe two]
- ⊠ Hair supplies
- ⊠ Cologne/perfume
- ⊠ Snack food [in case room service is closed]
- ⊠ Bathrobes
- ⊠ Bottled water
- ⊠ iPod/CD player
- ⊠ Something leather
- ⊠ Champagne flutes
- ⊠ Cash [for tipping the bellhop]
- ⊠ Bible

Advice and Forewarnings
[what you might experience your first time]

GUYS: If this is your first time, don't make the evening about hitting the bull's-eye. Just take your time and explore your lady's body. Make the time as magical as you have dreamed it would be since you were a kid. Remember, this is the first time; it's going to take some time to perfect it. Too often first-timers get wrapped up in trying to hold on for dear life to the first bullet.

LADIES: Don't expect a first-time shooter to even come close to hitting the target. *He might get lucky.* But don't bet on it. He's young; more than likely there's another round or two in him before his cartridge is empty.

GUYS: Take it slow. This is especially important if your wife is a virgin. In fact, there's a pretty good chance she's going to be a little nervous about your penis going inside of her for the first time. This isn't always the case, but it is probable. Many times, the first insertion is painful and can often result in her bleeding. Don't freak out about this. It's normal. Just be gentle and let her lead the way. However, know this: Depending on your wife's tolerance for pain, there's a chance you might not be able to get it in. Don't worry; it will happen. It just might take some time. So be patient. Sometimes more foreplay—either through touch or oral—might help your wife's body relax and become readied for penetration. Also, this is where Astroglide personal lubricant might come in handy. But this isn't always a guarantee.

LADIES: Talk your man through it. You know your body way better than he does at this point. Don't be afraid to tell him what you're feeling. He's probably as anxious as you are. Sometimes when guys get anxious, they push a little too hard.

So be vocal. Don't be embarrassed by the struggle it might take to get things gliding smoothly. If something doesn't feel right or if you're not able to handle the pain, tell him you're not going to be able to continue.

GUYS: If your wife is shy or quiet, you might need to help her feel comfortable voicing her feelings and concerns. According to most women, the first time hurts like crazy. So don't push or force an entry. Activate the safety on that gun of yours. If you do make safe passage, continue to follow her lead. Just because an "introduction" has been made doesn't mean it's time to dance. I promise that your wife will let you know when she's able to handle the two-step.

LADIES: You might try being on top. If the standard missionary [guy on top] position doesn't work for you, try being on top. This position gives you more control and allows you to advance at your comfort. Also, it's often much easier to find the angle that works for you. And believe me, your man won't mind you taking a turn at the wheel. In fact, he's apt to think it's hot.

BOTH OF YOU: Fun is the object of the game. Don't be overly serious. Laugh. Talk. Enjoy. Keeping up the communication will help you both resist the urge to allow tension to overwhelm your first attempt. Remember, this first time is

Most of us, at some time or another, have dreamed about our wedding night. If you're honest, you've probably spent a lot of time thinking about what the perfect "first night together" would entail. Maybe you've imagined something simple, like having rose petals on the bed [FYI: red rose petals stain sheets] or chilled champagne [sparkling grape juice for those who don't drink] on the bedside table. Or maybe you've imagined it big and dramatic, including a hot tub, strawberries and whipped cream, a fluorescent pink feather boa, and a pretend whip. Hey, I don't know what your sick minds might have dreamed up. But whatever you've fancied your wedding night to require, no doubt the room is an important facet to making your first night all it is meant to be. So in order to create the perfect atmosphere for lovemaking, make sure you plan ahead [at least three to four weeks prior to your big day] so you can make the environment everything you've always imagined. Just in case the old imagination has forgotten those creative concepts you dreamed about as an adolescent [or just last night], here are a few ideas to help you make the evening magical for you and your spouse.*

Have a massage table. Rent or borrow a real massage table for the evening. Add some fancy oils or lotions to the mix and BAM!, you've got yourself the makings of a very romantic massage experience. A massage table adds ease, flexibility, comfort, and sexiness to the ordinary massage. Plus, here's a bonus: You get another sturdy apparatus to play on. On top of that, a massage table will encourage you to take your time and treat your spouse to the best massage of his or her life. Make it hotter: Wear just a towel around your waist or body.

A votive is your romantic friend. A votive is the small, round candle your mom used to heat up her potpourri when you were a kid. Trust me on this one: Buy at least one hundred of those little things. And then, while your lover is in the bathroom prepping himself or herself to become a love machine, make several hearts or spell words on the floor of your room with the votives. Once the candles are lit, your new spouse will walk out of the bathroom into a romantic glowing love shack. [Just be sure you don't put them close to anything that

---

* For those who are married, use these ideas for a special occasion like Valentine's Day, an anniversary, or when you just feel like getting lucky [I mean, blessed].

might burn, and know where the fire extinguisher is!] Make it hotter: Add a couple drops of your favorite food coloring to the votive before lighting. As the candle begins to melt, your hearts and words will become bright and colorful. And if you're a guy, your wife will be completely overwhelmed with your attention to detail.

Have a theme. Okay, so a theme could either make or break the evening. I don't recommend you dress up like Obi-Wan or Princess Leah and have Star Wars memorabilia scattered around the room. You don't want to feel like you're having sex for the first time [or for the first time *again*] in a ten-year-old's bedroom. Perhaps the theme could be sixteenth-century art or "black and white" or something your spouse finds irresistible. Once you decide your theme, the sky is the limit. Use your imagination and do as much as your budget will allow [without going overboard]. Gaudy is not romantic. With the perfect theme, you'll create a playground worth remembering that both you and your spouse will enjoy. Make it hotter: Dress up as Darth Vader. *Kidding.* But seriously, a costume might be hot.

Re-create your husband or wife's dream. Sometime after the two of you are engaged, nonchalantly bring up the question, "Have you ever dreamed about our wedding night?" Whatever he or she says, re-create it to the best of your ability. And make it a surprise. How special would it be if on your wedding night, your new spouse walks into a room that is exactly like he or she had dreamed of? He or she will probably look at you and ask, "You were actually listening that day?" And then you can look back and coyly say, "Umm, well, most of it anyway." Make it hotter: Add little hints of your dream to it, too. This way you'll make sure your new spouse realizes you're not completely selfless.

HINT: If you're staying at a hotel or bed-and-breakfast, the hotel concierge service will usually be willing to help you plan the perfect evening. So take advantage of their expertise. The biggest thing is this: Don't become so overwhelmed with the details of the room that you lose focus on what the evening is really all about.

about the experience of being naked together, exploring the hot parts of each other's bodies that you're not too familiar with, and, if possible, becoming one. It's not about being perfect. But the experience will still seem perfect. And rest assured, if you're faithful in pursuing sexual exploration and growth, sex will continue to become hotter and more pleasurable.

Don't Get Dysfunctional About Dysfunction

Guys, even though you're young and vibrant, you might suffer from a short bout with erectile dysfunction before you turn thirty-five. This can happen for various reasons: medication, anxiety or stress, bad moods, serious medical problems, or even the flu. First off, if you do get caught with your pants down and your manhood not willing to stand up, don't stress about it. I know this is difficult, but how you think about this actually affects the problem. Take a day or two off from sex, and then try again. If you stress about it, you're apt to make things even more complicated. If the condition continues, you will want to see a doctor. More than likely, it won't be anything serious.

Of course, those of you who have been sexually active in the past know all of this already. So your first time *again* might be a little different from what is described above. Or it might very well be similar. Wedding-night sexual experiences are all different. So no one should take the above information as a guarantee but more as something to think about. The most important facet is to focus on each other. Enter into this experience with abandon. The ecstasy is found in being together — truly together — for the first time.

Practical Wisdom About Sex and Marriage

Robert Irwin travels around the country speaking to Christian men [and sometimes women] about God's role of sex inside the marriage union. Like most Christians, Irwin has always known that sex was ordained by God to bring a husband and wife together as "one flesh." In his book *Sexual Skill for the Christian Husband*, he says, "My family and church told me that sex was created by God and that within the proper context of marriage, it would be an exciting, intense and 'spiritual' event; an activity that would bring a married couple closer, physically, emotionally and spiritually." But that was *not* his experience. In fact, in their thirteen years of marriage, his wife had never experienced an orgasm. At age thirty-nine, a frustrated Irwin set out on a journey to discover God's "art" of sexuality. For more than a year and a half, he studied sex from a spiritual, mental, emotional, and physical standpoint. According to him, he figured it out and wrote it down in book form. In fact, his book, an online-only book, is one of the best-selling e-books of all time. I spoke with Irwin about what a man and a woman need to know before

How Many Times Do Married Couples Have Sex in a Year?

FACT: According to surveys by the condom company Durex, the worldwide average for married couples having sex is 103 times per year.[1]

they get married. In conclusion to this chapter about married sex, I thought his words were rather appropriate. [Please note that this interview has been edited down for clarity. Again, just in case this book gets chosen as Oprah's book of the month, I want everything to be upfront and honest.]

MPT: When a couple is having a problem with sexual intimacy, is it usually a *sexual* problem they're experiencing, or is it something else that's affecting their love life?

IRWIN: Matthew, the biggest thing that I have learned in my role as a "pseudo sex expert" is that most sex problems within a marriage are not really sex problems; they are relationship problems. It's difficult to have a good sex life if two people aren't getting along. A couple whose relationship is solid can find tremendous value in a good sex guide. But if a couple's relationship isn't solid or positive, even amazing sex won't help much. Sex alone will not make a bad relationship good.

MPT: In your opinion, what do you believe is the most important information a young couple should know regarding sex prior to walking down the aisle together?

IRWIN: As a Christian couple, it's important they understand that God created sex for their pleasure and to bring them closer, not just for procreation. They should also clearly understand that sex [within marriage] is an obligation and a duty, not an optional feature. Scripture is very clear on this point. Also, that the things that make sex great are essentially the same things that make the relationship great: selfless pursuit of your partner's best interest and pleasure, open and honest communication, patience and complete acceptance, etc.

MPT: What's the biggest misconception about sex among young Christian couples? And how can it be remedied?

IRWIN: Sadly, many have this subconscious perspective that sex is supposed to be something "less" for Christian couples. My remedy? First off, know and understand that God invented sex. Within his boundaries [within marriage], God expects sex to be an earth-shattering, soul-welding, sensual, and amazing experience. It should be frequent and filled with variety and passion. They should also know that there is no conflict between holiness and passion/sensuality for Christian married couples.

MPT: You've written a book for Christians about "good sex," which might imply that a good number of Christians have "bad" sex. Do Christian couples have bad sex?

IRWIN: In my experience, there are few real distinctions to be made between Christian and non-Christian couples. In most respects [divorce, adultery, sexual satisfaction] the statistics are exactly the same. What I will say is that when a Christian couple actually treats each other as the Scriptures direct us to, their relationship and sex life can be more amazing, in my opinion, than is possible with non-Christian couples because they have the additional spiritual connection aspect to their relationship and sexual activities. I don't think Christian couples capture that very real distinction.

MPT: What's the most common mistake Christian men make when having sex?

IRWIN: *[Laughs]* Matthew, probably the biggest mistake most men make is not realizing that their wives are on a different physiological path during sex. A guy is easily stimulated and brought to climax within a few moments, while most women require between fifteen and twenty-five minutes of foreplay/stimulation before they can achieve climax. This is not because they are less interested in sex [or in their husband]; it is a physiological fact. That's a huge difference.

MPT: Is there one "secret" that most men miss about their penis?

IRWIN: Men should realize that the glans [the ridge around the head of the penis] is the most sensitive location on their penis; it is equivalent in some ways to the woman's clitoris. Consequently, if they are looking to either speed up or delay their climax, they should either pay careful attention to or avoid this part of their penis. If they master this, they will be able to control their sexual stamina. Just read my book. *[Laughs]*

MPT: Is there a "secret" most women miss about their vagina?

IRWIN: Women need to recognize that their vagina is not intended to be a passive sexual organ. It is designed by God to be an amazing, very effective, active sexual organ. When women utilize their vaginas in this active way [gripping, pulling] it dramatically increases the pleasure for both them and their husbands.

MPT: Why is it important for husbands and wives to discuss each other's sexual needs?

IRWIN: For one, good sex is one more opportunity to demonstrate a concern and selfless desire to please your spouse. I think it's critical that husbands and wives discuss each other's sexual needs. Honestly, Matthew, it is no more or less critical than any other area of the marriage.

MPT: What should Christians do if they are married to someone who isn't enjoying sex?

IRWIN: First, they should pray about it. God is the true healer of all situations. Second, they should attempt to communicate to their spouse how they are feeling. If their spouse is not open to such a discussion, a pastor or other spiritual adviser should be consulted. Sexual activity

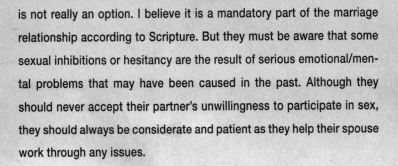

is not really an option. I believe it is a mandatory part of the marriage relationship according to Scripture. But they must be aware that some sexual inhibitions or hesitancy are the result of serious emotional/mental problems that may have been caused in the past. Although they should never accept their partner's unwillingness to participate in sex, they should always be considerate and patient as they help their spouse work through any issues.

MPT: At the beginning of your book, you talk a lot about God's idea of pleasure. What do you think sex tells us about the nature of God?

IRWIN: God is passionate, creative, and has a sense of humor. God endorses our entire beings, our bodies included. And God is "pro-pleasure" as long as it is within his proscribed boundaries.

If you would like to know how to find Robert Irwin's book about sex for Christian husbands, please e-mail me. It's perhaps one of the most helpful books I've read on the topic.

WOW. That was a really good section. Was it good for you? Yeah, same here; I think I need a break.

A Holy and Healthy Sexual Life Comes Down to This

[your heart]

Never lose a holy curiosity.

— Albert Einstein

One of the hardest parts about writing this book has been the advice and suggestions I have been given from people [mostly friends] who know I'm writing it. Let me tell you, some of the ideas I have received have been some real ring dingers. [Yes, I'm surprised, too, that I just used the term *ring dinger*. Oh gosh, there I go again. Puke. But for some reason, I can't go back and delete it. I should, but I just can't.]

Anyway, telling some of your best friends that their sex advice sucks is difficult to do. You have to be ultrasensitive to both their spiritual and sexual feelings. Insulting either a person's sexual or spiritual ego is bad enough, but when you could potentially shoot both down at the same time, you have to *really* tread carefully. I've had to look at some of my closest friends and say, "Thanks for your idea, but I don't think it will fit what I'm doing with this book."

One of my friends looked at me like I had just kicked his preacher in the crotch.

**I'm happy to be almost done.
All I need now is to nail the conclusion.**

I'm not sure if you're aware of this, but because this is a Christian book about sex, there's an unspoken formula I'm supposed to follow for this last section. I guess I assumed you might already know about the rules regarding the conclusions of Christian sex books since you've probably read a Christian sex book or two before. In case you're not aware of the formula, the last section is where I'm supposed to make sure you're fully aware of your Christian sexual responsibilities. Yes, I know I've already discussed these things throughout the book. But it's a book about sex from a Christian perspective; overkill is definitely part of the equation.

I feel somewhat obligated to comply.

Between you and me, it's not a difficult formula; it's not like it's quadratic or anything. Frankly, following the formula would probably make my job as a writer simpler.

Most Conclusions of Christian Best Sellers Follow This Formula:

1. Remind your readers what you've proclaimed in your book.
2. Prove again biblically that all you have said is indeed true.
3. Give them some direction on how they can apply this to their daily lives.
4. Dismount with a full double twist of inspiration. No bounce on the landing.

That's how I'm supposed to conclude this book. And all the really great Christian best sellers follow this formula. Lucky for you, the chances of this book becoming a best seller are probably as good as Karl Rove's chances of becoming super cool.

In light of those chances, I hope it won't bother you if I don't follow the formula.

So welcome to this sex book's conclusion. I hope you like it. If a sex book's conclusion were half as satisfying as the concluding moments of sex, I'd be pretty certain you would like it. But for your sake, I hope it's nowhere close to being that good. ✿ And for those of you who aren't supposed to know how good that is, ignore that last sentence.

Okay, on with the conclusion. I realize you've been reading the conclusion for the last three and half minutes. But all of the paragraphs prior to this one have been unnecessary filler. Trust me, my publisher didn't charge you for the filler. It was free.

Sex Begins with the Heart — Final Thoughts

When it comes to sex, I have received a great deal of advice over the years. Christians like giving advice about sex. It's comparable to their love of small groups and Max Lucado. In other words, sex advice [giving and getting] is just a part of being evangelical.

Unfortunately, not all the advice is good. I've heard bad advice. And no doubt I've given bad advice, too. Once in a while though, I've gotten great words of wisdom from people regarding sex.

A youth pastor friend of mine, Dennis Kirkland, is never shy about telling me his opinion. He's one of those guys who has either a good story or a good theory about almost anything. Once in a while, I think his words are genius.

On one such occasion about seven years ago, the two of us were up late at night [I lived with him and his wife for about a year] talking about something sex-related. I told him about a book I was reading, one that detailed the latest Christian method to pursuing a pure mind. As I shared the author's thoughts with Dennis, his facial expression fell from one of interest to that of utter exasperation.

"Ah, Matthew, give me a break," said Dennis. "That book sounds like another load of processed Christian crap."

Dennis always has a way with descriptions. Although his not-so-subtle approach would sometimes rub my then easy-to-offend Christian faith the wrong way, I always listened.

"That's just another 'purity' formula aimed at twentysomethings, right?" asked Dennis.

"Perhaps," I said with a grin.

"Matthew, people don't find purity in a formula. That's true if you're sixteen or sixty-five. Scripture makes it rather clear that human methods don't make us holy or pure or more acceptable in the eyes of God."

Dennis didn't shut up for almost twenty minutes about his thoughts on the "formula." I'm glad he didn't. That talk was one of the most healing conversations [despite it being one-sided] I had experienced during those difficult months/years of sexual temptation.

During that time, chasing a formula was so tempting. I believe it is for a lot of us, no matter our stories or desires. It's so easy to simply follow a formula. Lots of Christians try to create formulas for holy and healthy sexual living. It's just a natural response, I suppose.

However, formulas do not work.

Back in section 1, I asked you to write down your sexual history. You remember that, right? And I'm assuming [and you know what that does] you took the time to do it. Take another look at what you wrote down.

Some of you, after having read sections 2, 3, and 4, may need to alter your list a bit. Perhaps your opinion about your sexual history has changed, or maybe something you believed to be a positive thing now looks more like a negative, or vice versa. [If you do have things to change, go ahead and do it; I'll wait here. Oh, it's no problem. I have nothing better to do than wait for you to finish your sexual history list. I'm actually being serious; I don't have anything better to do.]

As you read over the list, consider for a moment how many of the situations in your life you've attempted to fix with a formula. Whether your list includes a battle with lustful thoughts, a struggle with porn, failure at purity, bad sexual education, your parents' divorce, or any other problem you've had, have you ever tried a formula or a "game plan" to solve these things?

Maybe you don't know what I'm talking about when I say "formula." Let me explain.

When I was twenty-five and knee-deep in my struggle with pornography, I went to a large men's event with my church. Thousands of men from various faith backgrounds crammed into one huge coliseum.

One vivid memory I have of that weekend was that of a group of men, maybe five hundred or so on the main floor, who during every intermission would begin chanting, "I love Jesus, yes I do. I love Jesus, how 'bout you?"

It gets worse.

I was asked to join in. So I did. I joined a big group of men in the highest balcony and helped them shout out a reply. We stood up proudly and yelled, "WE LOVE JESUS, YES WE DO . . ."

Some Christians love their chanting.

During the two-day event, a preacher randomly came out on stage and riled up the fifty thousand men with a little game of "repeat after him." "A GODLY MAN IS A MAN OF GOD!" he yelled over the loudspeaker. Every man in the audience echoed his phrase. "AND A MAN OF GOD IS A GODLY MAN!" he continued. The crowd echoed him again.

We probably said that statement sixty times during that two-day event. That same preacher later came out and talked to us about lust, porn, and sexual immorality.

"Men of God," he preached, "I am offering you a solution for the lust you're battling in your daily lives." The preacher then went on to present a strategy for purity that included daily prayer, weekly meetings with others who struggled, a book and workbook that you would do with a group, and a purity commitment card that you were supposed to sign.

The preacher, toward the end of his talk, presented his own purity story, one that included no TV after ten p.m., no Internet usage during certain times of the day, confessional meetings with his pastor, and other points I cannot remember.

That's a formula. A formula is a spiritual procedure that promises an end result. Most of the time these types of spiritual equations sound amazing. In fact, when one is "on fire for Jesus," these formulas can make us believe they're helping, that we're becoming purer by following the list of things to do. However, despite creating some good habits, these lists do little for the cause of purity in one's life and more often than not create a "standard" toward which people feel compelled to strive.

Christian culture is rather obsessed with formulas. Formulas make us feel like we're in the process of taking control of our problems or that we're on the path toward utter spiritual ecstasy. Heck, sometimes they make us feel like we're actually in control. Some of the best advice I can offer is this: Stop following formulas.

Formulas feel good for a time, but eventually you realize they actually suck. It's kind of like what you felt when you first watched *Star Wars: The Attack of the Clones*. You liked it, right? However, when you went back to watch it a second time on DVD, you realized that the "Lucas" hype had altered your movie-going perspective. After the second viewing, you ended up walking away thinking, *Wow, I thought that was a lot better the first time.* Sadly, it wasn't. However, you won't truly be convinced of *Attack's* utter mess of a plotline until you see it a third time. Then the truth gets revealed. *Why?* Because *Star Wars* fans are addicted to the "Force's" propaganda just like Christians are addicted to following formulas in pursuit of holy and healthy sexual living.

And just like going against the mind-set that says, "Anything George Lucas creates is amazing" is a difficult road to travel, tearing yourself away from the habit of formulas is equally challenging. A person's constant need for a formula is a hard habit to break. It's especially difficult when "formula addiction" promises the pathway to sexual fulfillment, healing, purity, and contentment.

Who doesn't want to feel all of that?

But why do we feel the need to join a club in order to experience sex the way God intended us to? I'm inclined to believe fear keeps us running back to a routine.

In his book *Water from Stone: When "Right Christian Living" Has Left You Spiritually Dry*, Christian therapist and speaker M. Wayne Brown writes, "Our demand for control and guaranteed blessing through Christian formulas is not a manifestation of faith, but of fear. If [we] are looking for a system of faith that will solve the dilemmas of parenting, courtship, or career, the system will most certainly break down."[1]

Brown describes the Christian formula as "a pragmatic and programmatic approach to faith that is so convincing, so pervasive, so widely accepted, that we are often impotent to resist its influence."[2]

I think in many instances, formulas are an insult to the gospel because they take the focus off of Jesus and put it on a person's ability [and, in many instances, inability] to perform. Sometimes the focus gets put on the mistake. Either way, following a formula can screw up a person's thinking.

I don't know about you, but when my heart and mind are consumed with thinking about my mistakes or inabilities, the feelings of guilt and anxiety aren't too far behind. Guilt and anxiety cripple a person's spiritual life, and they cripple a person's ability to be holy and healthy, too. It's difficult for a follower of Jesus to breathe in the gospel when he or she is trying to outfox temptation on his or her own.

Well, what you probably haven't thought about before is this: The gospel improves your sex life.

Am I taking some creative license here?

I don't think so. If God created sex and wants me to be pleasured by sex within marriage, then why wouldn't his gospel affect my sex life?

I believe it does.

I've learned this to be true about sex, purity, and the questions I have about sex and purity. If you desire to pursue a holy and healthy sex life, build your "sexual foundation" on Jesus. In other words, make him the center of your life.

This sounds cliché to some of you.

But like every other facet of a Christian's life, our sex lives—no matter if we're single, at the beginning of a dating relationship, engaged, or married—are dependent upon whether or not we're surrendering to Jesus and his will for our lives.

Forgive me while I get a wee bit cheesy for a moment.

➤ When you're in your dorm secretly looking at pornography, JESUS is your way out.
➤ If you've ever been sexually abused, JESUS can fill you with the hope you need in the midst of your situation.
➤ When your married sex life is less than perfect, JESUS is the spark.
➤ If you're not sure your dating motives are pure, JESUS is your fact check.

If we build our holiness or healthiness around anything other than JESUS, holy and healthy sexual living becomes out of the question.

I know this is a rather simple truth. And it doesn't answer all of your questions.

If it makes you feel any better, it doesn't answer all of mine, either.

But don't all the good topics come with a lot of questions, at least the ones really worth discussing? Over the years, I've learned that if God had meant for us to know *everything*, he would have told us everything. Some of God's greatest gifts are those he hasn't given us in full color, those left with black-and-white spaces meant for us to color as he designed.

Sex is one of those topics. It's peculiar, strange, and not fully colored in.

Of course, God does leave us with instructions on how to color — he tells us that our hearts need to be pure.

Our sexuality begins in the heart. Jesus teaches, "From the heart come evil thoughts, murder, adultery, all other sexual immorality, theft, lying, and slander" (Matthew 15:19, NLT). A person surrendered to Jesus has a clean heart. You can't earn something like that. We try to, but we can't. But that doesn't leave us without hope.

Jesus says this:

"I am telling you these things now while I am still with you. But when the Father sends the Counselor as my representative — and by the Counselor I mean the Holy Spirit — he will teach you everything and will remind you of everything I myself have told you.

"I am leaving you with a gift — peace of mind and heart. And the peace I give isn't like the peace the world gives. So don't be troubled or afraid." (John 14:25-27, NLT)

The best thing you can do for your sex life is to pursue a pure heart through becoming intimate with Jesus. Period. That's not a formula. I can't put that in the form of a funny list. I don't have a punch line to share. It's just simple advice from someone who knows what you're going through.

OKAY. THE END. KIND OF.

Five Questions to Consider Before You Close the Book

1. What does holy and healthy mean to you?

2. Have you ever tried a formula in pursuit of holy and healthy living?

3. What area of your "sex" life is the most challenging?

4. Can you look back on your past and see where the mistakes you made were heart related?

5. How does the truth that comes from Jesus affect the heart?

Alternate Ending

[just in case this book
does become a best seller]

1. This book was about sex.
2. Sex is in the Bible — a lot.
3. You should get married before engaging in sex.
4. Does doing a back flip in the middle of my living room make this information more exciting? If I were to stick the landing, would that help?

The happiness of a man in this life does not consist in the absence but in the mastery of his passions.

— Alfred, Lord Tennyson

[Cue laugh track.]

A nun, a preacher, and a prostitute walk into a bar together . . .

[A whole bunch of stuff that I'm not allowed to mention happens during this part.]

But eventually, they all read this book, confess their sins, and begin serving poor people in Africa.

[See what can happen when you read this book?]

Notes

Section One: Growing Up Christian, Learning About Sex

1. Jennifer M. Parker, "The Sex Lives of Christian Teens," *Today's Christian*, March/April 2003, http://www.christianitytoday.com/tc/2003/002/7.28.html.
2. "The Sexual Shadows — Trends," *Group Magazine*, January 2, 2004, 18.

Section Two: The Bible and Sex

1. Denys Turner, *Eros and Allegory: Medieval Exegesis of the Song of Songs* (Cambridge, MA: Cistercian Publications, 1995).
2. Ronald L. Ecker, "Rahab the Harlot," in *And Adam Knew Eve: A Dictionary of Sex in the Bible* (Hodge & Braddock, 1995), see http://www.hobrad.com/andr.htm#RU.
3. Ronald L. Ecker, "Ruth: At His Feet Until Morning," in *And Adam Knew Eve: A Dictionary of Sex in the Bible* (Hodge & Braddock, 1995), see http://www.hobrad.com/andr.htm#RUTH.

Section Three: Welcome to the Real World

1. "Morality Continues to Decay," *Barna Research*, November 3, 2003.
2. Hugh Ross, *Creation as Science* (Colorado Springs, CO: NavPress, 2006), 156.
3. "The Masturbation Guide," www.afraidtoask.com/masturbate/History.htm.
4. "The Masturbation Guide."
5. "The Masturbation Guide."
6. D. E. Greydanus and B. Geller, "Masturbation: Historic Perspective," *New York State Journal of Medicine*, November 1980, 91–92.
7. "The Masturbation Guide."
8. "The Masturbation Guide."
9. "Men Only — Personal Issues," crosswalk.com, http://forums.crosswalk.com/Men_ONLY_-_Personal_Issues/forumid_69/tt.htm.
10. Dale Kaufman, "Is Masturbation a Sin?" http://www.youthspecialties.com/articles/topics/sexuality/masturbation.php.
11. Kaufman.
12. "Pornography Statistics," *Family Safe Media*, http://www.familysafemedia.com/pornography_statistics.html.
13. For more information on being a good accountability partner, check out Jon Walker, "Accountability: There Are No Lone Ranger Christians," pastors.com, http://www.pastors.com/article.asp?ArtID=7058.
14. "STI Fast Stats," smartersex.org, http://smartersex.org/index.asp.

Section Four: Marriage and Sex

1. "The Global Sex Survey 2005," Durex, http://www.durex.com/cm/gss2005results.asp.

Section Five: A Holy and Healthy Sexual Life Comes Down to This

1. M. Wayne Brown, *Water from Stone: When "Right Christian Living" Has Left You Spiritually Dry* (Colorado Springs, CO: NavPress, 2004), 184.
2. Brown, 14.

About the Author

MATTHEW PAUL TURNER is the best-selling author of *The Christian Culture Survival Guide* and *Provocative Faith*. Before he began speaking and writing full-time, he served as editor of *CCM* and music and entertainment editor for Crosswalk.com. He and his wife, Jessica, live in Nashville, Tennessee. To find out more about Matthew, visit his website at www.MatthewPaulTurner.com.

"Right now, all over the world, the child relief organization World Vision is helping to save the lives of millions of children. Whether a country is crazed with famine, or by AIDS or by natural disaster, World Vision is there reaching out to individuals and communities with things like physical, emotional and spiritual help. World Vision continues to be the hands and feet of Jesus throughout the world."

— Matthew Paul Turner